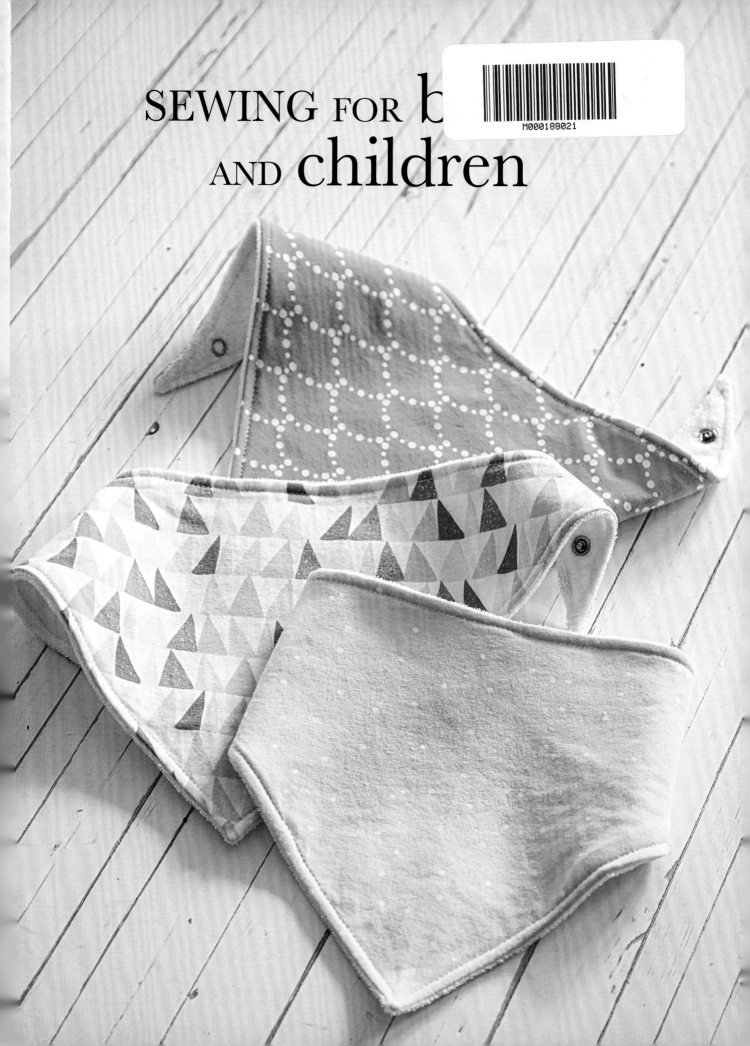

SEWING FOR b

AND children

M000188021

SEWING FOR babies AND children

25 beautiful designs for clothes and accessories for ages 0–5

Laura Strutt

CICO BOOKS

LONDON NEW YORK

www.rylandpeters.com

Dedication

To my sister, Jenny Coomber, and her wonderful tribe of children who make me happy and proud to be an Aunty!

Published in 2017 by CICO Books
An imprint of Ryland Peters & Small Ltd
20–21 Jockey's Fields   341 E 116th St
London WC1R 4BW   New York, NY 10029

www.rylandpeters.com

10 9 8 7 6 5 4 3 2 1

Text © Laura Strutt 2017
Design, illustration, and photography © CICO Books 2017

The author's moral rights have been asserted.
All rights reserved. No part of this publication may be reproduced, stored in a retrieval system, or transmitted in any form or by any means, electronic, mechanical, photocopying, or otherwise, without the prior permission of the publisher.

A CIP catalog record for this book is available from the Library of Congress and the British Library.

ISBN: 978 1 78249 423 2

Printed in China

Editor Sarah Hoggett
Designer Sarah Rock
Photographer Emma Mitchell
Stylist Jo Sawkins
Illustrator Carrie Hill

Art director Sally Powell
Head of production Patricia Harrington
Publishing manager Penny Craig
Publisher Cindy Richards

Note: All instructions in this book contain both standard (imperial) and metric measurements. Please use only one set of measurements when cutting out and sewing, as they are not interchangeable.

contents

introduction

I love working on small garments and mini projects. Not only are they, more often than not, quick and easy to make, but they also use only small amounts of fabric, so you can use up all those pretty remnants in your stash or splash out on some of those pricier fabrics you've had your eye on! Experienced stitchers and beginners alike will love how quickly these smaller-sized garments come together to create your own custom collection of baby and children's clothes.

For this book I wanted to create a collection that would be both easy to sew and fun to wear. The projects include either templates or full-size pattern pieces, so you can remake your favorites as many times as you like. Check the size chart below to establish the correct size for your child. Each project includes full instructions alongside stunning illustrations to help keep you on the right track. Not only that, there are also lots of handy tips and tricks throughout to help you achieve results you can be really proud of.

Unlike store-bought clothes, these garments—from ruffle bloomers and harem pants for babies to everyday t-shirts and shorts for younger children—are worked up in a collection of fun contemporary prints and colors, and include lots of ideas for customizing, embellishing, and personalizing your creations, so you can add some individuality to your makes. Many of these designs are unisex, and can be worked in different colorways, or with small adjustments to make them suitable for boys or girls.

The book is arranged into three sections—Babywear, Children's Clothes, and Accessories—so whether you are picking out items for a new arrival, for your own little one or to make and give as gifts, or making clothes for a toddler, you'll be sure to find plenty of inspiration. I have had such a wonderful time designing this collection of garments and accessories. I hope that you have just as much fun stitching up your own collection of handmade items for the little ones in your life!

Happy sewing!
Laura

SIZE CHART

	0–3 months	3–6 months	6–12 months	1–2 years	2–3 years	3–4 years	4–5 years
HEIGHT	26 in./66 cm	28 in./72 cm	29 in./76 cm	32½ in./83 cm	38½ in./98 cm	41 in./104 cm	43½ in./110 cm
CHEST	17½ in./44 cm	18 in./46 cm	18½ in./47 cm	19 in./48 cm	20½ in./52 cm	22 in./56 cm	23 in./58 cm
WAIST	16 in./41 cm	16½ in./42 cm	17½ in./44 cm	18 in./46 cm	19½ in./50 cm	20½ in./52 cm	21½ in./54 cm

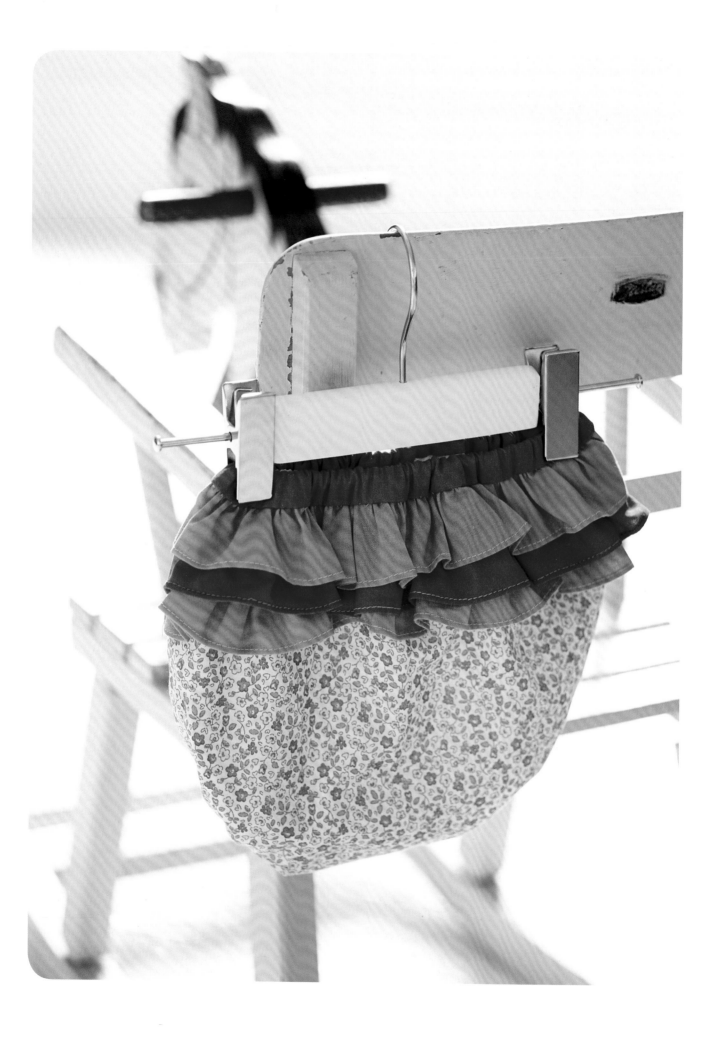

babywear

There is no warmer way to welcome a new baby than with a selection of handmade garments, and the ones in this chapter are both comfortable and practical. Made in super-soft fabrics such as jersey and designed to be easy to slip on and off, these are the perfect first garments for new babies.

cloth crib shoes

These soft cloth baby shoes are the perfect first footwear for little ones—the elasticated opening makes them easy to slip on, comfortable to wear, and holds them snugly in place. As the shoes require only small amounts of fabric, they are ideal for using up those pretty remnants from your stash.

YOU WILL NEED

- Fat quarter of print cotton in each of two contrasting designs (fabrics A and B)
- Fat quarter of solid cotton in a complementary shade (fabric C)
- 39 x 45 in. (100 x 115 cm) lightweight iron-on interfacing
- 20 in. (50 cm) elastic, ¼ in. (5 mm) wide
- Coordinating thread
- Sewing machine
- Iron
- Dressmaking scissors
- Pins
- Large-eyed needle or bodkin
- Seam ripper

SIZES

The patterns are for ages 0–3, 3–6, and 6–12 months.

PATTERN NOTES

The template for the soles of the shoes needs to be turned over to create both left and right shoes.

Take a ¼-in. (5-mm) seam allowance throughout.

PATTERN PIECES REQUIRED

Shoe upper
Sole
Shoe back

1 Following the manufacturer's instructions, apply iron-on interfacing to the wrong sides of both the print cotton fabrics. Using the pull-out patterns, cut two shoe uppers from fabric A and two shoe backs from fabric B. From fabric C cut four soles (turning the pattern over to get a left and a right sole), two shoe uppers, and two shoe backs. Do not zig-zag the edges, as this will create unwanted bulk when the shoes are assembled. Set all the sole pieces aside.

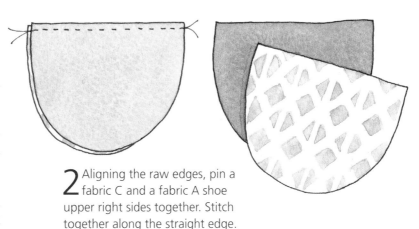

2 Aligning the raw edges, pin a fabric C and a fabric A shoe upper right sides together. Stitch together along the straight edge. Press the seam open.

MAKE IT YOURS

For more active toddlers, make a more robust version from a lightweight leather or suede. Be sure to select the correct sewing needle and thread for your machine if you are working with leather.

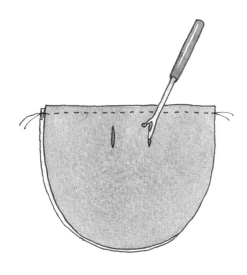

3 Fold along the seam line so that the wrong sides of the fabrics are together. Working ¼ in. (5 mm) from the fold line, topstitch along the upper (straight) edge. Using a seam ripper and following the guides on the pattern piece, make two small slits in the solid fabric C only; this will provide a casing for the elastic later. Repeat steps 2 and 3 to make the second shoe upper. Set both aside.

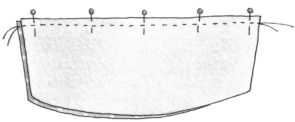

4 Aligning the raw edges, pin a fabric B and a fabric C shoe back right sides together. Stitch together along the straight edge. Press the seam open. Fold under ¼ in. (5 mm) to the wrong side along both short edges and press.

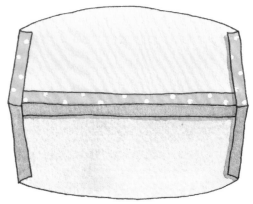

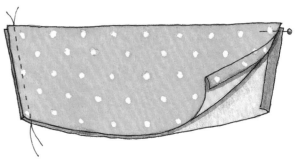

5 Fold the shoe back along the seam line and press, making sure that the folded sections along the short sides are neatly tucked inside. Press and pin in place. Topstitch down both short sides ¼ in. (5 mm) from the edge. Repeat steps 4 and 5 to make the second shoe back.

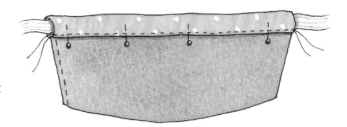

6 Along the top straight edge of each shoe back, fold ⅝ in. (1.5 cm) of the fabric B side over onto the fabric C side, and press in place. Cut two 10-in. (25-cm) strips of elastic. Place one inside each fold, making sure that the elastic is pushed right to the inside of the fold so that it won't be close to the stitching line; there should be a small length of elastic protruding at each side. Pin and stitch the fold in place.

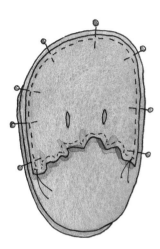

7 Place a corresponding pair of fabric C soles wrong sides together and treat as one piece. With right sides together, pin and stitch a shoe upper to the sole. Repeat with the second shoe upper and sole.

✂ TIP *Keep the stitches neat around the curved sections by sewing slowly; this will ensure that all the layers are included when sewing. If you prefer, you can always work the seam in two parts: start from the center point of the curve and work outward, then return to the center and work the second part of the seam out in the opposite direction.*

✂ TIP *Check the sizing by slipping the shoes on before securing the elastic; this will help you to get a snug fit that won't slip off but won't be too tight or uncomfortable on little feet.*

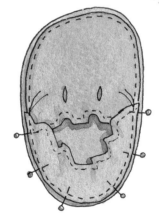

8 With right sides together, pin then stitch a shoe back to the sole. Repeat with the second shoe back and sole. Trim the seam allowance around the shoes and turn them right side out.

9 Using the bodkin, draw the elastic protruding from one side of the shoe through both the small slits in the front of the shoe upper lining, being careful not to pull it out of the casing. Check the length of the elastic needed, overlap the two ends by 1–2 in. (2–5 cm), and box stitch (see page 124) the ends of the elastic together. Tuck the elastic back inside the casing to finish.

finishing Snip away all remaining thread ends to neaten.

rounded bib

This soft, rounded bib is a feeding-time staple: the combination of a printed cotton fabric and soft toweling makes it both cute and super absorbent—ideal for keeping the little one clean when at the table. You can use the same pattern to make an even easier and quicker bib without a mini pocket on the front.

YOU WILL NEED
- 10-in. (25-cm) square of stretch toweling
- 10-in. (25-cm) square of print cotton fabric
- 8 x 10in. (20 x 25 cm) contrast print cotton fabric for the pocket
- 10-in. (25-cm) square of lightweight, iron-on stretch interfacing
- 60 in./150 cm bias binding if making with pocket, or 48 in./120 cm without pocket
- Coordinating thread
- Sewing machine
- Iron
- Dressmaking scissors
- Pins
- Knitting needle

SIZE
Approx. 7 x 7 in. (19 x 19 cm)

PATTERN NOTE
Take a ³⁄₈-in. (1-cm) seam allowance throughout, unless otherwise stated.

PATTERN PIECE REQUIRED
Bib template on page 125

1 Following the manufacturer's instructions, apply iron-on interfacing to the wrong side of the stretch toweling.

2 Make a paper pattern using the template on page 125. Fold the main print cotton fabric and stretch toweling in half, wrong sides together. Pin the pattern on the fold and cut one from stretch toweling and one from print cotton. Use the lower portion of the pattern piece to cut two pockets from the contrast print, pinning on the fold as before.

> **MAKE IT YOURS**
> Mix and match different prints to make a coordinating set of bibs.

3 Zig-zag stitch all around each piece to secure the raw edges. Press each piece.

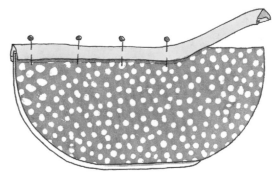

4 Pin the two pocket pieces wrong sides together, aligning the raw edges. Cut an 8⅝-in. (22-cm) length of bias binding and slip it over the straight top edge of the pocket to conceal the raw edge. Press neatly and pin in place. Select a longer stitch (⅛ in./3 mm) on your sewing machine and topstitch along the binding, ¼ in. (5 mm) from the fold, to secure it in place. Pin the completed pocket to the bib front and treat as one piece.

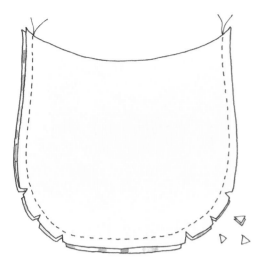

5 Pin the front and back bib pieces right sides together, aligning the raw edges. Set your stitch length back to normal. Stitch around the sides of the bib, leaving the top edge (the neckline) unstitched. Carefully snip small V-shapes into the seam allowance along the curved sections of the bib to ease the curve when turning through, being very careful not to cut through the stitching.

6 Turn the bib right side out through the neck opening, using a knitting needle to push out the curves. Press to neaten. The pocket will now be on the lower front of the bib.

7 Fold the remaining bias binding in half to find the center point. Matching this point to the center front of the neckline, slip the binding over the neckline and pin it in place. Pin outward from the center point in both directions, using an iron to help ease the binding around the curve and making sure that the width of the binding is the same on both sides all the way around.

TIP *These bibs use only small amounts of fabric, so they are great for using up remnants from your stash. If you are using printed motifs, take the time to position the pattern piece over the fabric to make the best use of the motifs.*

8 Select a longer stitch (⅛ in./3 mm) on your sewing machine and topstitch along the entire length of the binding, including the ties, stitching ¼ in. (5 mm) from the fold.

finishing Snip away all remaining thread ends and press to neaten. Neatly knot the ends of the ties.

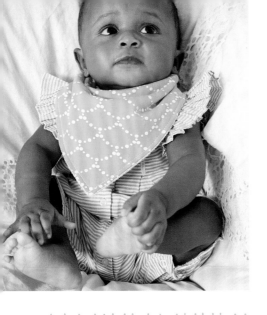

bandana bib

Keeping babies clean and dry when they are teething and weaning is a full-time job, but this bandana-style bib is made from ultra-soft jersey and teamed with stretch toweling, which means that it is not only comfortable for baby, but also easy to launder. The snap fastener makes it easy to replace throughout the day, so baby will not only look cute but will also stay clean and dry!

YOU WILL NEED

- 18-in. (45-cm) square of jersey fabric
- 18-in. (45-cm) square of stretch toweling
- 18-in. (45-cm) square of lightweight iron-on stretch interfacing
- Two snap fasteners
- Coordinating thread
- Sewing machine with a stretch stitch and ballpoint/jersey needle
- Iron
- Dressmaking scissors
- Pins
- Knitting needle
- Hand sewing needle

SIZE

Bib measures: 18½ x 12½ x 12½ in. (47 x 32 x 32 cm)
Neck opening measures approx. 14 in. (35 cm)—this can be customized

PATTERN NOTE

Take a ⅜-in. (1-cm) seam allowance throughout, unless otherwise stated.

PATTERN PIECE REQUIRED

Bib template on page 124

1 Following the manufacturer's instructions, apply iron-on interfacing to the wrong side of the jersey fabric.

2 Make a paper pattern using the template on page 124. Fold the jersey and the toweling fabrics in half, wrong sides together. Pin the bib pattern on the fold of the jersey and carefully cut out. Repeat with the toweling fabric. Press both pieces flat.

3 Pin the pieces right sides together, aligning all the edges. Insert a ballpoint needle into your sewing machine and select a stretch stitch. Stitch the two pieces together, leaving a 3-in. (8-cm) gap in the center of one straight side. Carefully clip away the corner points and trim down any bulky sections of seam allowance. Along the long, curved edge, snip small V-shapes in the seam allowance to ease the curve when turning through, being very careful not to cut through the stitching.

MAKE IT YOURS
Why not add a brightly colored toweling for the backing and select a contrast thread for the finishing topstitching?

TIP *For tips on working with stretch fabrics, see pages 109 and 110.*

4 Turn the bib right side out through the gap and use a knitting needle to push out the points. Around the gap in the stitching, carefully push the seam allowance inside the bib, press to neaten, and pin in place. Slipstitch the gap closed.

TIP *To make the bib multi sized, simply add a second snap fastener to give yourself the option of fastening it in different places.*

5 Select a longer stitch (⅛ in./3 mm) on your sewing machine and topstitch around the bib ¼ in. (5 mm) from the edge, pivoting at the corner points.

6 Stitch one half of a snap fastener approximately 2 in. (5 cm) (or your preferred measurement to accommodate the baby's neck) from the point on one long edge of the jersey side. Attach the second part of the fastener to the corresponding section of the other point, on the toweling side.

finishing Snip away all remaining thread ends and press to neaten.

tie-top beanie

Keep little ones cozy with this sweet beanie hat. Made from ultra-soft jersey, it's comfortable enough to keep baby warm all day.

YOU WILL NEED
- 12 x 16 in. (30 x 40 cm) jersey fabric
- 12 x 16 in. (30 x 40 cm) lightweight, iron-on stretch interfacing
- Coordinating thread
- Sewing machine with a stretch stitch and ballpoint/ jersey needle
- Iron
- Dressmaking scissors
- Pins
- Knitting needle
- Hand sewing needle

SIZES
The patterns are for ages 0–3, 3–6, and 6–12 months.

PATTERN NOTES
For fabrics with larger prints, you may need to increase the fabric amount to accommodate the motifs and to allow for matching prints where required.

Take a ⅜-in. (1-cm) seam allowance throughout, unless otherwise stated.

PATTERN PIECE REQUIRED
Beanie

1 Following the manufacturer's instructions, apply iron-on stretch interfacing to the wrong side of the jersey fabric.

2 Place the beanie pattern on the jersey, pin it in place, and carefully cut out. Repeat to cut a second identical piece.

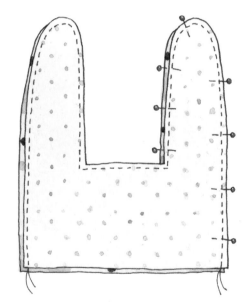

3 Pin the two pieces right sides together. Insert a ballpoint needle into your machine and select a stretch stitch. Starting at the bottom of one side of the hat, stitch up the side, around the top and ties, and back down the second side, leaving the bottom edge unstitched.

TIP *Applying a fusible interfacing with a slight stretch is a great way to give the fabric a little more stability, which makes it easier to stitch without losing its shape or changing the way the fabric handles too much.*

TIP *If you are working with a printed fabric, try to match the prints at the front and back of the hat to give a really professional finish.*

MAKE IT YOURS
You can increase or decrease the size of this hat by simply enlarging or reducing the size of the hat template to accommodate the baby's head measurements.

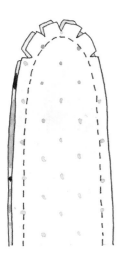

4 Carefully snip small V-shapes into the seam allowance around the curved sections, being very careful not to cut through the stitching. Turn the hat right side out and use a knitting needle to ease out the upper sections of the ties.

5 Measure the circumference of the base of the beanie, then cut a strip from the remaining jersey fabric to this length plus ¾ in. (2 cm) x 2½ in. (6.5 cm). Fold it in half widthwise, with wrong sides together. Aligning all the raw edges, pin the band to the bottom edge of the hat. Where the ends of the band overlap, place one inside the other and tuck in the raw edges of the outer piece. Stitch in place.

6 Fold the band down, so that the fold in the strip forms the bottom edge of the beanie, and press the seam allowance up toward the body of the hat.

finishing Snip away all remaining thread ends and press to neaten. Knot the upper tie sections together.

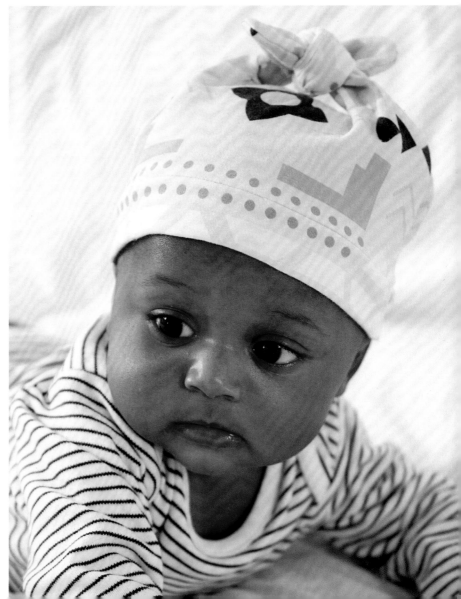

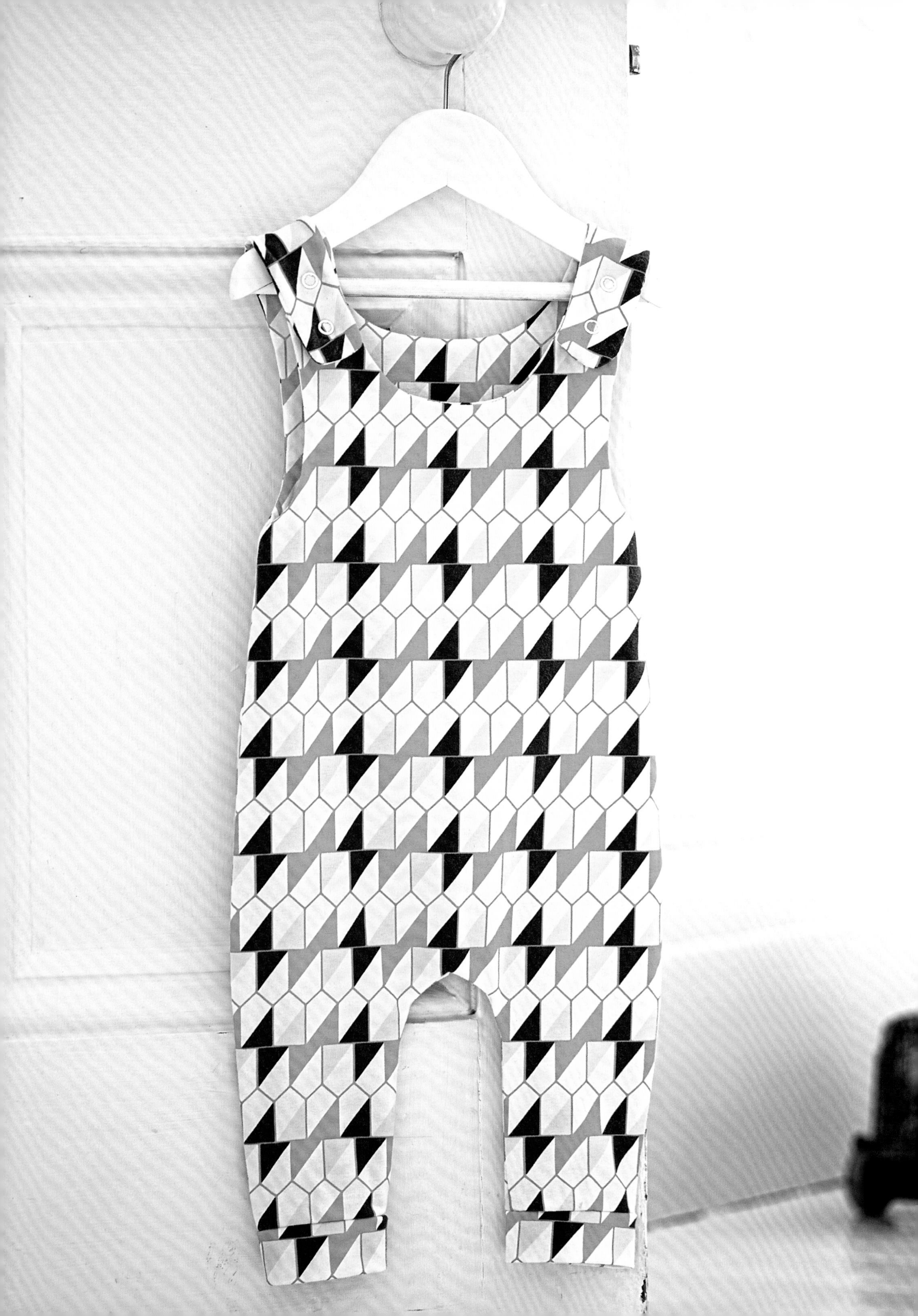

YOU WILL NEED

- 30 in. (75 cm) jersey fabric, 60 in. (150 cm) wide
- 4 snap fasteners
- Coordinating thread
- Sewing machine with a stretch stitch and ballpoint/ jersey needle
- Iron
- Dressmaking scissors
- Pins

SIZES

The patterns are for ages 0–3, 3–6, and 6–12 months.

PATTERN NOTE

Take a ⅜-in. (1-cm) seam allowance throughout, unless otherwise instructed.

PATTERN PIECES REQUIRED

Romper back
Romper front
Back facing
Front facing
Cuff

baby romper

This fun romper suit is perfect for little girls and boys alike, with snap fasteners making it quick and easy to slip on and off. The roomy design makes it perfect for concealing bulky diapers (nappies), and it can be worn over a long-sleeved vest for added warmth.

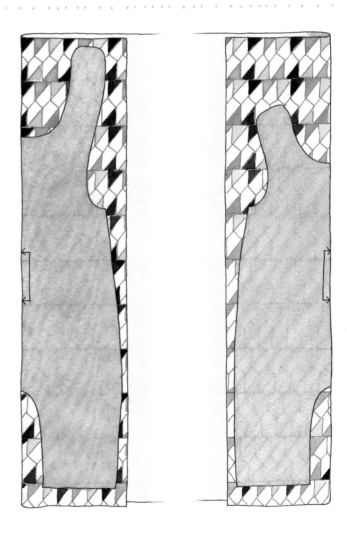

MAKE IT YOURS

Why not use a contrasting color of jersey for the cuffs or add a patch pocket to the front?

1 With wrong sides together, fold the selvages of the jersey fabric in toward the center, just far enough to be able to place the whole of the front and back pattern pieces on the folds. Cut one front and one back.

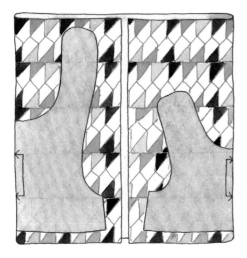

2 Cut the front and back pattern pieces as marked to make patterns for the front and back facings. Fold the side edges of the remaining fabric in to the center. Place the facing pattern pieces on the folds and cut one front and one back facing. Cut two cuff pieces.

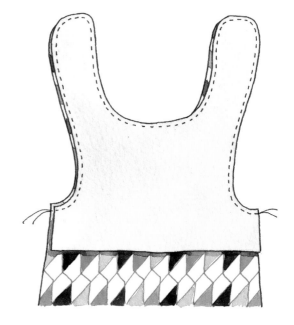

TIP *Although it isn't essential, taking the time to work around each piece of knit fabric with a zig-zag stitch does prevent the raw edges from curling under and makes it easier to piece all the elements together.*

3 Zig-zag stitch around the outer edges of all of the pieces to secure the raw edges. Press each piece.

4 Pin the romper front and front facing right sides together, aligning the raw edges. Insert a ballpoint needle in your machine and select a stretch stitch. Taking a ¼-in. (5-mm) seam allowance, stitch the facing to the front, starting at one underarm curve and stitching over the straps and bib section and back down to the other underarm curve. Leave the side seams unstitched. Repeat with the romper back and back facing.

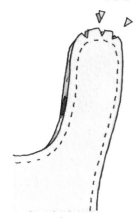

5 Snip small V-shapes in the seam allowance along the curved sections of the straps and neckline to ease the curve when turning through, being very careful not to cut through the stitching. Turn right side out and press.

6 Open the romper back and back facing out as far as the stitching done in step 4, and put them right side up on your work surface. Open out the romper front and front facing in the same way, then lay them right side down on top of the back pieces, aligning the side edges and ensuring that the join at the underarm meets neatly. Pin together. Starting at the ankle and working up to the underarm and then along the facing, work a single straight seam along one side of the romper. Repeat on the other side. Press the seams open.

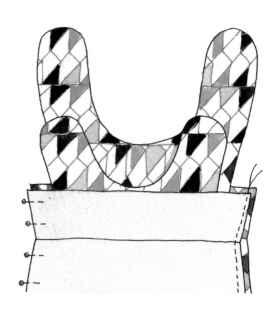

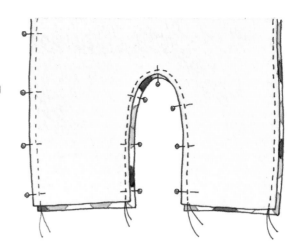

7 With the right sides still together, align the inside leg seam on the front and back and pin in place. Starting at the bottom of one leg, stitch up the leg, across the crotch, and back down the other leg. Press the seam open.

8 With right sides together, fold the cuffs in half lengthwise and stitch the short ends together to form a loop. Press the seams open. Fold the loops in half widthwise, with the seam on the inside. With the romper suit right side out, and aligning the cuff seams with the inside leg seams, slide the cuffs onto the legs and pin in place, aligning the raw edges. If possible, remove the extension part of the machine and work with the free arm. Stitch around the lower part of the leg to secure the cuffs in place. Fold the cuffs down, and press the seam allowances up, toward the romper.

9 Stitch one half of two snap fasteners to each of the back strap pieces, positioning the first one ⅝ in. (1.5 cm) from the bottom of the strap, centered on the width of the strap, and the second one ⅝ in. (1.5 cm) above it. Stitch the second part of the fasteners to the front straps, making sure they align.

finishing Snip away all remaining thread ends and press to neaten.

✂ TIP *Get the fit just right by slipping the romper onto the recipient to mark the placement for the snap fasteners. Adding in an additional set at a different height gives the garment a little more "growing room."*

- 1 yd (90 cm) jersey fabric, 60 in. (150 cm) wide
- 16 in. (40 cm) elastic, ¼ in. (5 mm) wide
- Coordinating thread
- Sewing machine with a stretch stitch and ballpoint/jersey needle
- Iron
- Dressmaking scissors
- Pins
- Hand sewing needle
- Safety pin

SIZES

The patterns are for ages 0–3, 3–6, and 6–12 months.

PATTERN NOTE

Take a ⅜-in. (1-cm) seam allowance throughout, unless otherwise stated.

PATTERN PIECES REQUIRED

Body front
Body back
Front neckband
Back neckband
Sleeve
Cuff

MAKE IT YOURS
Work the back and front neckbands in a contrasting color of jersey.

envelope-neck babygrow

There is nothing quite as adorable as a baby in a babygrow! This retro style features a sack-style lower section, meaning that it has done away with the fussy lower legs and fasteners, so it is an ideal project for novice stitchers. It has a wide envelope neckline, so it is easy to put on and, for emergency changes, can be pulled down the baby's body, rather than dragging any mess over baby's head and face!

1 Fold the selvages of the fabric in to meet in the center. Place the pattern pieces on the folds and cut one body front, one body back, one front neckband, and one back neckband. From the remaining fabric, cut two sleeves and two cuffs. Set aside the fabric until you are ready to cut the elastic casing (in step 8) Transfer the pattern markings to the fabric (see page 121).

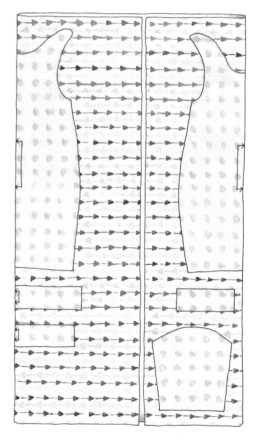

2 Zig-zag stitch around all the pieces to secure the raw edges. Press each piece.

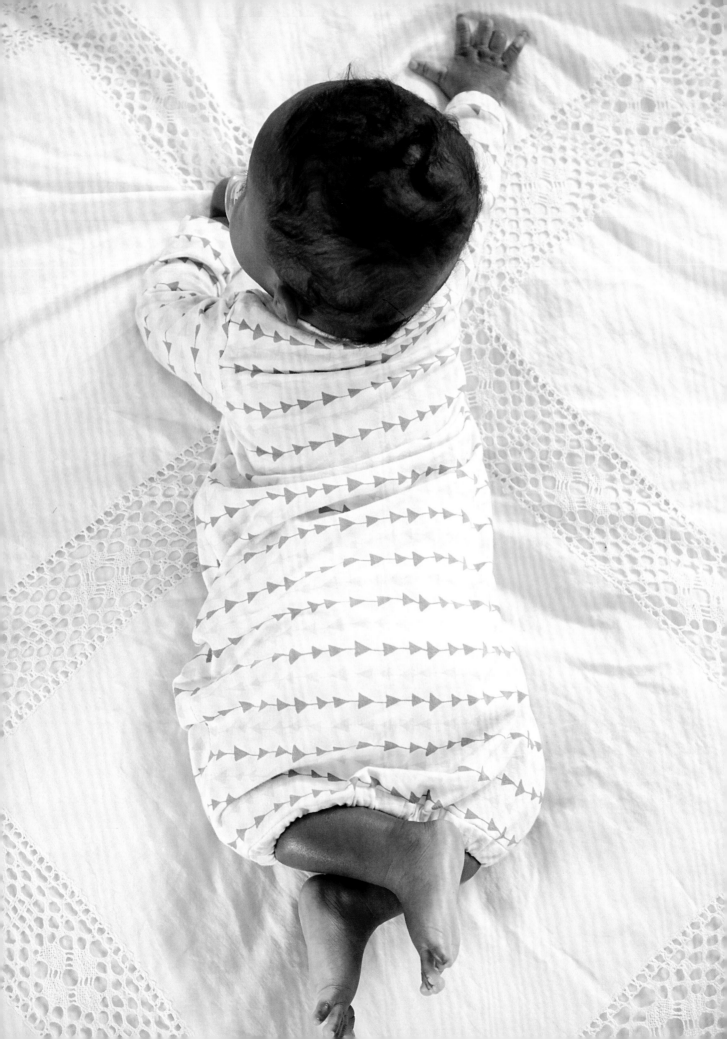

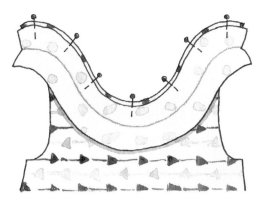

3 With wrong sides together and aligning the long raw edges, press the front neckband in half, then open it out again. With right sides together, pin the neckband along the neckline of the body front, easing it across the full length of the neckline. Pin in place. Insert a ballpoint needle into your sewing machine and select a stretch stitch. Taking a ¼-in. (5-mm) seam allowance, sew the neckband in place.

TIP *The neckline may stretch slightly once it is cut, so you will need to ease the neckbands. Work by pinning from the center first and moving outward, pressing with an iron as you work for a really neat fit.*

4 Re-fold the neckband along the center crease and bring the remaining fabric of the strip to the wrong side of the body front. Fold under the raw edges of the neckband and pin it in place. Set your machine to a straight stitch and stitch the neckband in place, stitching ⅛–¼ in. (3–5 mm) from the folded edge. Repeat steps 3 and 4 to attach the back neckband to the body back.

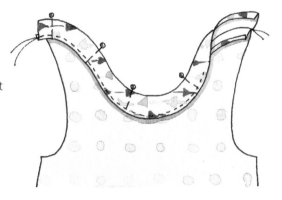

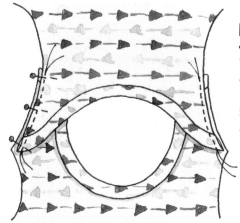

5 Lay the body front right side up on your work surface. Using the pattern markings, overlap the body back on top to create the shoulder seams and pin in place. This forms the neckline. Set your machine back to a stretch stitch and stitch the seams on each side, taking a ¼-in. (5-mm) seam allowance.

6 With wrong sides together, fold the cuffs in half lengthwise and press. Aligning the raw edges, pin the folded cuffs to the right side of the sleeves. Stitch in place, taking a ¼-in. (5-mm) seam allowance. Press the cuffs down and press the seams up toward the sleeves.

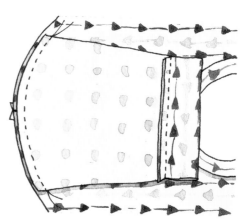

7 Open out the garment and lay it right side up. With right sides together, pin the sleeve over the shoulder seam stitched in step 5; the sleeve head (the rounded upper section) will align with the curve of the shoulder of the garment. Stitch in place. Repeat for the second sleeve.

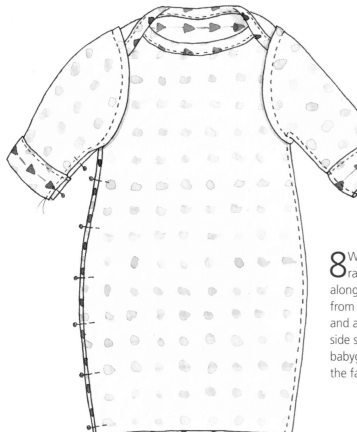

8 With right sides together and aligning the raw edges, pin the front and back together along the underarm and side seams. Starting from the bottom and working up to the armpit and along to the end of the cuff, stitch the side seams. Measure around the bottom of the babygrow and cut a 1½-in. (4-cm) wide strip of the fabric that is this length plus 1 in. (3 cm).

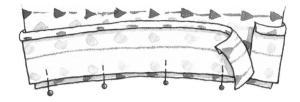

9 With wrong sides together and aligning the long raw edges, fold the casing strip in half and press to create a center fold. Open out, then press under ¼ in. (5 mm) to the wrong side along one long raw edge. Pin the unpressed edge of the strip around the lower edge of the body and overlap the raw ends. Stitch in place, taking a ¼-in. (5-mm) seam allowance.

10 Fold the pressed edge of the casing over to the inside of the babygrow and slipstitch around, leaving a 1–2-in. (3–5-cm) gap. Attach the safety pin to one end of the elastic and feed it through the casing, overlapping the ends by 1–2 in. (3–5 cm). Box stitch (see page 124) to secure. Slipstitch the gap in the casing closed.

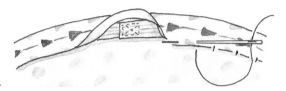

finishing Snip away all remaining thread ends and press to neaten.

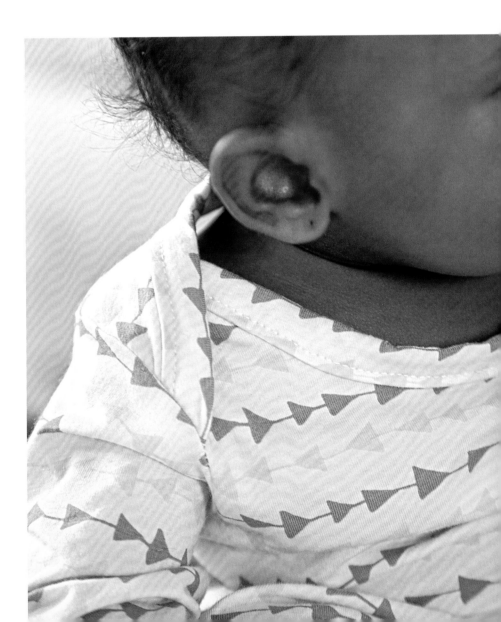

baby harem pants

These slouchy baby leggings are made from a super-cozy jersey that is perfect for both nap time and crawling around in. The dropped crotch style means that they can accommodate the extra bulk of a diaper (nappy) in style!

YOU WILL NEED

- 20 in. (50 cm) jersey fabric, 60 in. (150 cm) wide
- 10 in. (25 cm) contrast jersey fabric, 60 in. (150 cm) wide
- 14 in. (35 cm) elastic, 1 in. (2.5 cm) wide
- Coordinating thread
- Sewing machine with a stretch stitch and ballpoint/jersey needle
- Iron
- Dressmaking scissors
- Pins
- Hand sewing needle
- Safety pin

SIZES

The patterns are for ages 0–3, 3–6, and 6–12 months.

PATTERN NOTE

Take a ⅜-in. (1-cm) seam allowance throughout, unless otherwise stated.

PATTERN PIECES REQUIRED

Pants
Cuff
Waistband

1 With wrong sides together, fold the selvages of the main jersey fabric in to meet in the center. Place the pants pattern pieces on each fold in turn and cut to create one front and one back. From the contrast jersey fabric, cut two cuffs and one waistband. Zig-zag stitch all around each piece to secure the raw edges. Press each piece.

TIP *Take the time to position the pattern pieces before cutting to accommodate any motifs; this will enable you to match the patterns along the seams for a truly professional finish.*

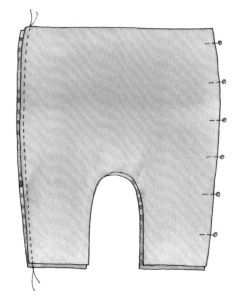

2 With right sides together and aligning the raw edges, pin the front and back pieces together. Insert a ballpoint needle into your machine and select a stretch stitch. Beginning at the waist on one side, stitch down the side seam as far as the ankle, then repeat on the other side. Then sew the inside leg and crotch seam, working from one ankle round to the other. Leave the waist and both ankle sections unstitched.

TIP *Although knit fabrics don't fray like woven ones, working a line of zig-zag stitching over the raw edge helps to hold them flat, making it much easier to join them together.*

MAKE IT YOURS
This pattern can be easily scaled up or down for larger or smaller children—just remember to adjust the fabric amounts accordingly.

3 With right sides together and aligning the two short edges, fold the cuff strips in half lengthwise. Pin, then stitch the short edges together to form a loop. Press the seam open. Turn the loop right side out, then fold it in half widthwise, with the seam on the inside. With the pants right side out and aligning the raw edges and the cuff seams with the inside leg seams, slide the cuffs onto the legs of the pants and pin in place. If possible, remove the extension part of the machine and work with the free arm. Stitch around the lower part of the legs to secure the cuffs in place.

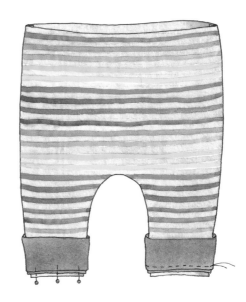

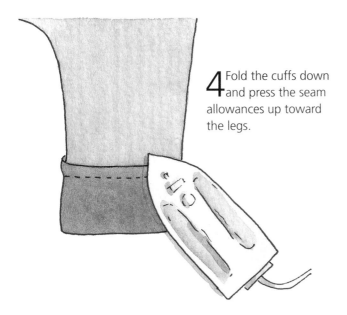

4 Fold the cuffs down and press the seam allowances up toward the legs.

TIP *Try not to stretch the fabric as it is drawn through the feed dogs, as this will create uneven seams.*

5 Attach the waistband (see page 124), aligning the seam in the waistband with one of the side seams and leaving a 1½ in. (4-cm) gap at one side seam. Using the safety pin, insert the elastic, box stitch the ends together (see page 124), then slipstitch the gap in the waistband closed.

finishing Snip away all remaining thread ends and press to neaten.

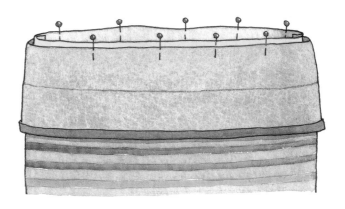

ruffle bloomers

These bright bloomers are great for slipping under tunics and dresses and make a great cover-up for crawling babies on the move! The addition of cute, colorful ruffles makes them even more fun—but if you prefer something simpler, or want to make them for a little boy, simply omit the ruffles.

YOU WILL NEED

- 30 in. (75 cm) print cotton, 44 in. (112 cm) wide
- 30 in. (75 cm) lining cotton, 44 in. (112 cm) wide
- Contrast solid cottons for the ruffles, waistband, and leg casings:
  Light pink: 4 x 44 in. (10 x 112 cm)
  Dark pink: 10 x 44 in. (25 x 112 cm)
- 36 in. (90 cm) transparent, elastic polyurethane tape, ¼–⅜ in. (5–9 mm) wide
- 36 in. (90 cm) elastic, ¼ in. (5 mm) wide
- Coordinating thread
- Sewing machine
- Iron
- Dressmaking scissors
- Pins
- Rolled hem foot
- Safety pin or bodkin
- Hand sewing needle

SIZES

The patterns are for ages 0–3, 3–6, and 6–12 months.

PATTERN NOTE

Take a ⅜-in. (1-cm) seam allowance throughout, unless otherwise stated.

PATTERN PIECES REQUIRED

Bloomer front
Bloomer back

1 Fold the print cotton and lining cotton in half, wrong sides together, and cut one bloomer front and one bloomer back on the fold from each fabric. For the waistband and leg casings, measure the circumference of the leg and waist and cut dark pink strips to these measurements plus ¾ in. (2 cm) (for the seam allowances) and 1½ in. (3.5 cm) deep. For the ruffles, cut two light pink and one dark pink strip, twice the width of the bloomer back at the waist plus ¾ in. (2 cm) and 1¾ in. (4.5 cm) deep.

2 Attach a rolled hem foot to your sewing machine and select a suitable stitch (refer to your sewing machine manual for guidance). Apply a rolled hem (see Tip, right) to one long edge of each ruffle strip.

TIP *A rolled hem foot is used to replace the standard presser foot to create neat and narrow hems. The foot has a curved section of metal at the front, which catches the fabric and gently rolls it prior to stitching. Place the fabric wrong side uppermost and ease the edge of the fabric into the curved section of the foot, then select a straight machine stitch. The foot will create an even roll of fabric along which the stitches are worked, giving a small, neat finished hem.*

MAKE IT YOURS

Omit the ruffles and make in a brushed cotton or a soft toweling for a more traditional diaper (nappy) cover.

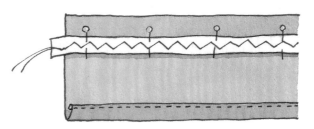

3 Cut a 12-in. (30-cm) length of transparent elastic polyurethane tape and pin it to the unhemmed edge of a ruffle strip ⅜ in. (1 cm) below the raw edge. Attach a standard machine foot to your machine and select a zig-zag stitch. Stitch the first ½ in. (1 cm) or so of elastic to the strip. Pull the elastic out to the full length of the ruffle strip and work a line of stitching to secure it to the strip. This will create a gather in the fabric. Continue stitching until you get to the last ¾ in. (2 cm) of fabric, release the tension on the elastic, and secure the remaining length. Repeat with the remaining ruffle strips.

4 Zig-zag stitch around the edges of bloomer front and back pieces in both the print cotton and the lining cotton to secure the raw edges. Press each piece.

TIP *Transparent PU tape is a clear or opaque sew-in elastic which draws up to create quick, neat ruffles. Be sure to stitch along the center of the tape for the neatest results.*

5 Pin the bloomer front and back lining pieces right sides together, aligning the straight side edges. Set your machine to a straight stitch and stitch each of the side seams in turn. Then pin and stitch the crotch seam. Press the seams open.

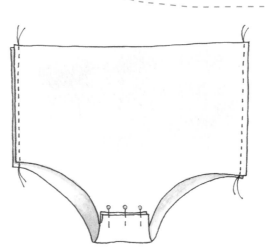

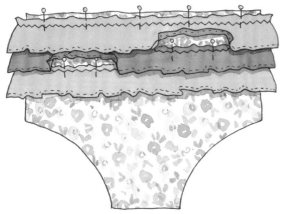

6 Now stitch the ruffle strips to the right side of the main fabric bloomer back. Align the raw edge of a light pink ruffle strip with the top raw edge of the back and pin it in place. Pin the dark pink ruffle ⅜ in. (1 cm) below the first and the second light pink ruffle ⅜ in. (1 cm) below that. There will be a small amount overhanging at each side. Taking a ¼ in. (5-mm) seam allowance, stitch the ruffles in place.

7 Repeat step 5 with the front and back main fabric pieces, smoothing the ruffles as needed. Trim off the excess ruffles at each of the side seams in line with the seam allowance. Press the seams open.

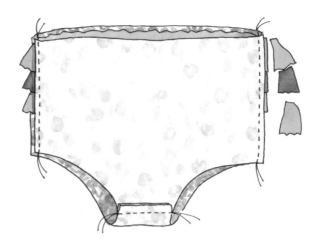

8 With wrong sides together, aligning the legs and waist edges, slip the lining inside the main fabric bloomers. Attach the waistband (see page 124), aligning the seam in the waistband with one of the side seams and leaving a 1½ in. (4-cm) gap at the center back. Insert the elastic, box stitch the ends together (see page 124), and slipstitch the gap in the waistband closed.

9 Following the instructions for an elasticated waist on page 124, fold, press, and attach the leg casings, leaving a 1½ -in. (3-cm) gap when you slipstitch the casings to the inside of the bloomers. Cut a 4-in. (10-cm) length of elastic for each casing. Insert the elastic, box stitch the ends together (see page 124), and slipstitch the gap closed.

finishing Snip away all remaining thread ends to neaten.

CHAPTER 2
children's clothes

Toddlers and small children are full of energy and fun, and these garments are designed to be stylish for play, parties, or everyday wear. Dress things up with a Peter Pan collar dress or a smart bowling shirt, or keep it casual with retro-style dungarees or a pom-pom trimmed skirt.

envelope-neck t-shirt

Jersey T-shirts are super against delicate skin and the wider opening of an envelope neckline makes them easier to slip onto busy toddlers. This classic design is surprisingly simple to make and you'll want to whip up a collection in a range of your little one's favorite colors!

YOU WILL NEED

- 24 in. (60 cm) double-sided striped jersey fabric, 60 in. (150 cm) wide
- 8 x 32 in. (20 x 80 cm) solid jersey fabric
- Coordinating thread
- Sewing machine with a stretch stitch and ballpoint/jersey needle
- Iron
- Dressmaking scissors
- Pins
- Hand sewing needle

SIZES

The patterns are for ages 1–2, 2–3, 3–4, and 4–5 years.

PATTERN NOTE

Take a ⅜-in. (1-cm) seam allowance throughout, unless otherwise stated.

PATTERN PIECES REQUIRED

Front
Back
Neckband
Lower band
Sleeve

MAKE IT YOURS
Extend the length of the sleeves to make a long-sleeved design for the colder months.

1 Fold the selvages of the striped jersey fabric inward to accomodate the pattern pieces as shown. Cut one front and one back on the folds, and cut two sleeves. Cut two neckbands and one lower band from the solid jersey fabric. Transfer the pattern markings to the fabric (see page 121).

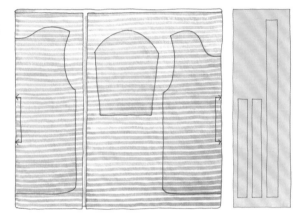

✂ **TIP** *Taking the time to position the pattern pieces before cutting will allow you to match the print—the stripes— across the seams for a more professional-looking finish.*

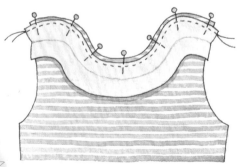

2 With wrong sides together and aligning the long raw edges, press the front neckband in half, then open it out again. With right sides together, pin the neckband along the neckline of the T-shirt front, easing it across the full length of the neckline. Pin in place. Insert a ballpoint needle into your sewing machine and select a stretch stitch. Taking a ¼-in. (5-mm) seam allowance, sew the neckband in place.

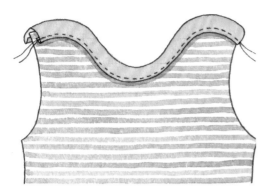

3 Re-fold the neckband along the center crease and bring the remaining fabric of the strip to the wrong side of the T-shirt front. Fold under the raw edges of the neckband and pin it in place. Set your machine to a straight stitch and stitch the neckband in place, stitching ⅛–¼ in. (3–5 mm) from the folded edge. Repeat steps 2 and 3 to attach the back neckband to the T-shirt back.

4 Lay the T-shirt front right side up on your work surface. Using the pattern markings, overlap the T-shirt back on top to create the shoulder seams and pin in place. Set your machine back to a stretch stitch and stitch the shoulder seams on each side, taking a ¼-in. (5-mm) seam allowance.

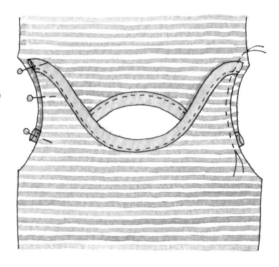

5 Open out the garment and lay it right side up. With right sides together, pin and stitch the sleeves to the joined front and back pieces along the shoulder seams.

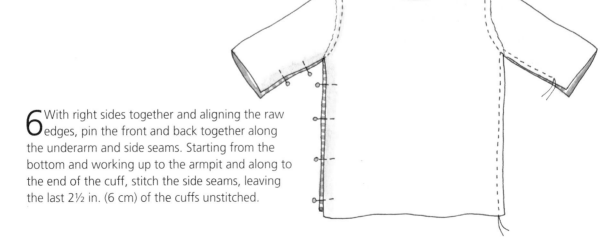

6 With right sides together and aligning the raw edges, pin the front and back together along the underarm and side seams. Starting from the bottom and working up to the armpit and along to the end of the cuff, stitch the side seams, leaving the last 2½ in. (6 cm) of the cuffs unstitched.

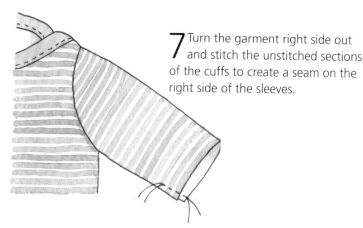

7 Turn the garment right side out and stitch the unstitched sections of the cuffs to create a seam on the right side of the sleeves.

8 Fold ⅜ in. (1 cm) over to the wrong side around the base of the sleeves and stitch in place. Turn up each cuff by 1 in. (2.5 cm) and then by another 1 in. (2.5 cm) and press.

✂ **TIP** *By working the lower part of the sleeve seam with the seam outermost, you can create neat turn-ups, ensuring that the seam allowances are not visible on the finished garment.*

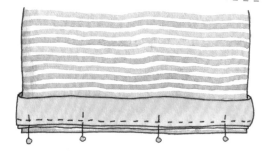

9 With right sides together and aligning the two short edges, fold the lower band strip in half lengthwise. Pin, then stitch the short edges together to form a loop. Press the seam open. Turn the loop right side out, then fold it in half widthwise, with the seam on the inside. With right sides together and aligning the raw edges and the seam in the loop with one of the side seams, pin and then stitch the strip to the bottom edge of the T-shirt, taking a ¼-in. (5-mm) seam allowance.

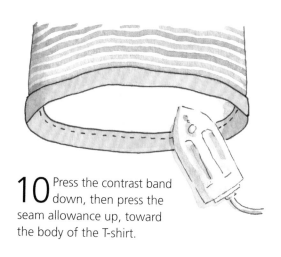

10 Press the contrast band down, then press the seam allowance up, toward the body of the T-shirt.

finishing Snip away all remaining thread ends and press to neaten.

peasant dress

The elasticated neckline and sleeves not only make this easy for little ones to slip on and off themselves, but also allow you to make adjustments to get the perfect, comfortable fit.

YOU WILL NEED

- 27½ in. (70 cm) main fabric print cotton, 60 in. (150 cm) wide
- 18 in. (45 cm) contrast print cotton, 44 in. (112 cm) wide
- 18 in. (45 cm) contrast solid cotton, 60 in. (150 cm) wide
- Transparent, elastic polyurethane tape
- 16 in. (40 cm) elastic, ¼ in. (5 mm) wide
- 16 in. (40 cm) grosgrain ribbon, ⅝ in. (1.5 cm) wide
- 6 in. (15 cm) grosgrain ribbon, ⅜ in. (1 cm) wide
- Coordinating thread
- Sewing machine
- Iron
- Dressmaking scissors
- Pins
- Safety pin
- Hand sewing needle

SIZES

The patterns are for ages 2–3, 3–4, and 4–5 years.

PATTERN NOTES

For fabrics with large prints, you may need to increase the fabric amounts to accommodate the motifs and to allow for matching prints where required.

Take a ⅜-in. (1-cm) seam allowance throughout, unless otherwise stated.

PATTERN PIECES REQUIRED

Dress
Sleeve
Contrast hem

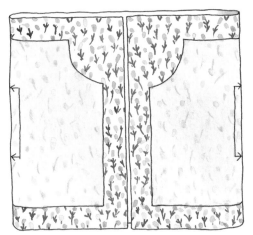

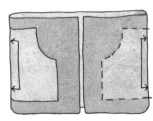

1 With wrong sides together, fold the selvedges of the main and contrast print fabrics in to meet in the center. Place the dress pattern on the folds of the main fabric print cotton and cut two dress pieces. Place the sleeve pattern on the folds of the contrast print fabric and cut two sleeves. Use the lower portion of the dress pattern to cut two contrast hem sections from solid cotton.

2 Zig-zag stitch around all the pieces to secure the raw edges. Press each piece.

MAKE IT YOURS

The dress can be made in a single fabric for a simpler style, or you can mix and match prints and solid cottons for the sleeves, dress, and contrast hem to create your own unique design.

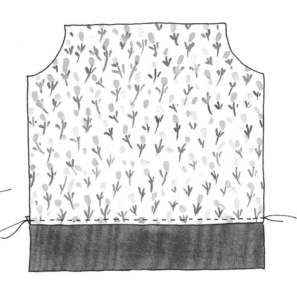

3 Set your machine to a straight stitch. With right sides together, pin and machine stitch the contrast hem along the bottom edge of the dress front. Press the contrast hem down and press the seam allowance up (toward the dress) on the wrong side of the main fabric. Select a longer stitch (⅛ in./3mm) on your sewing machine and topstitch along the bottom edge of the main print cotton, ¼ in. (5 mm) from the seam. Repeat to attach the contrast hem to the dress back.

✂ **TIP** *Take the time to press the fabrics and seams at each stage, as this will make it easier to join the pieces and give a much neater finish.*

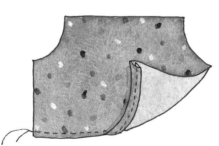

4 Fold under a double ¼-in. (5-mm) hem to the wrong side along the straight edge of each sleeve, and pin in place. Topstitch close to the fold to secure.

5 Set your stitch length back to normal. With right sides together and aligning the curves, pin and stitch the sleeves to the dress front around the armholes.

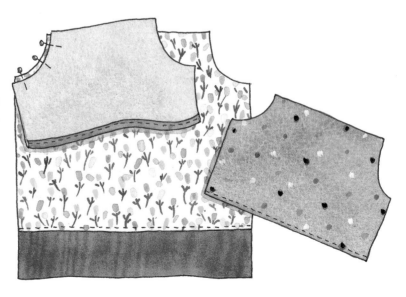

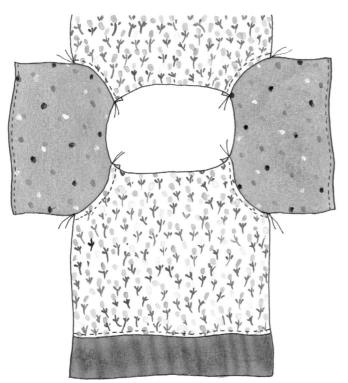

6 Repeat step 5 to attach the other side of each sleeve to the back of the dress. The dress front and back will now be joined together along the seams at the raglan sleeves. Press each seam of the raglan sleeves toward the dress. Select a longer stitch (⅛ in./3 mm) on your sewing machine and topstitch ¼ in. (5 mm) from the seam on the front and back dresses to secure the seam allowances.

7 Cut a piece of transparent elastic polyurethane tape two-thirds of the width of the sleeve and pin it in place, stretching the tape across the fabric. Work two lines of stitching down the elastic tape to hold it in place, then remove the pins. Repeat to elasticate the second sleeve in the same way.

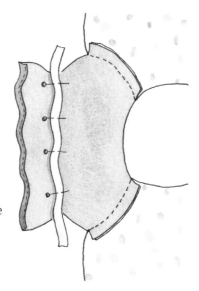

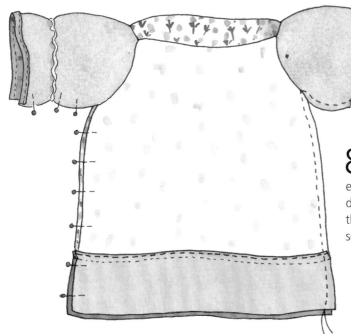

8 Pin the dress front and back right sides together, aligning the raw edges. Starting from the hem of the dress, stitch up the side and along the sleeve. Repeat with the other side seam. Press the seams open.

9 Fold under ⅝ in. (1.5 cm) to the wrong side around the entire neckline and press neatly. Tuck the raw edge under by ¼ in. (5 mm), press, and pin in place. Stitch around the neckline approximately ⅛ in. (3 mm) from the lower fold to create a casing, leaving 1–2 in. (3–5 cm) unstitched at the center back.

10 Attach the safety pin to one end of the elastic and feed it through the casing. Once the elastic is fed through, pull both ends out of the casing and overlap them by 1 in. (2.5 cm) to accommodate the child's head and neck measurements. Carefully box stitch the overlapped ends together (see page 124), then allow the elastic to slip back inside the casing. Slipstitch the gap in the casing closed.

TIP *You can adjust the size of the neckline by slipping the dress on the child and adjusting the elastic in the casing before stitching.*

11 Hem the dress with a double-turned ⅜-in. (1-cm) hem. Make a small loop from each ribbon and stitch another loop of the wider ribbon around them. Add ribbon tails of the wider ribbon behind, trimming the ends on the diagonal. Stitch in place at the neckline.

finishing Snip away all remaining thread ends and press to neaten.

button detail dress

This slip-on dress with simple tie straps is the perfect addition to a little girl's summer wardrobe. Big, bright, candy-striped buttons provide an eye-catching finishing touch, but are purely for decoration—so there are no fiddly buttonholes to sew!

YOU WILL NEED

- 28 in. (70 cm) solid cotton, 44 in. (112 cm) wide, for the bodice
- up to 17 in. (42 cm) striped cotton, 60 in. (150 cm) wide for the skirt (see step 1 for exact measurements by size)
- 3½ x 6 in. (8.5 x 15 cm) white cotton fabric, for the button placket
- 10 in. (25 cm) wide white rick-rack braid
- Three buttons, 1 in. (2.5 cm) in diameter
- Coordinating thread
- Sewing machine
- Iron
- Dressmaking scissors
- Pins
- Knitting needle
- Hand sewing needle

SIZE

The patterns are for ages 2–3, 3–4, and 4–5 years.

PATTERN NOTES

For fabrics with large prints, you may need to increase the fabric amounts to accommodate the motifs and to allow for matching prints where required.

Take a ⅜-in. (1-cm) seam allowance throughout, unless otherwise stated.

PATTERN PIECE REQUIRED

Dress bodice

1 With wrong sides together, fold the selvages of the bodice fabric in to meet in the center. Place the bodice pattern on the folds, flipping as necessary, and cut four pieces—two for the outer bodice and two for the lining. For the skirt, cut a rectangle of striped cotton measuring 15 x 51 in./16 x 52 in./17 x 53 in. (38 x 127.5 cm/40 x 130 cm/ 42 x 132.5 cm), depending on the size you are making.

MAKE IT YOURS
Why not make the dress in a single print cotton for a more classic design?

2 Zig-zag stitch around all the pieces to secure the raw edges. Press each piece.

3 Fold under and press ¼ in. (5 mm) to the wrong side along each long edge of the white cotton button placket and place the placket on the center front of one of the outer bodice pieces. Cut the rick-rack braid into two equal lengths. Tuck one piece under each side of the placket, so that only one wavy edge is showing, and pin in place. Select a long straight stitch (⅛ in./3mm) on your sewing machine and topstitch along each side of the placket ¼ in. (5 mm) from the edge. Sew three buttons onto the center front of the placket, spacing them evenly.

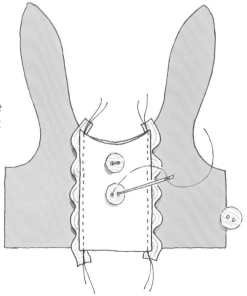

4 With right sides together and aligning the raw edges, pin one bodice lining piece on top of the bodice with the button placket. Set your stitch length back to normal and stitch around the upper section, starting at the top of the armhole on one side and ending at the top of the armhole on the other side. Repeat to stitch the other lining piece to the remaining outer bodice. Snip off the points at the ends of the ties and trim down any bulky sections of seam allowance. Along the curved sections of the ties and the neckline, snip small V-shapes in the seam allowance to ease the curve when turning through, being very careful not to cut through the stitching.

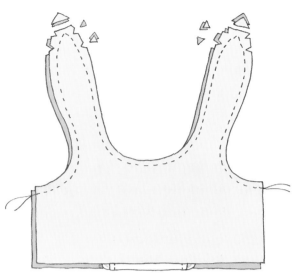

5 Turn the bodice pieces right side out, using a knitting needle to push out the points of the ties. Press to neaten.

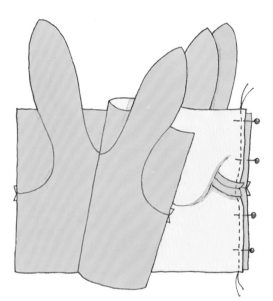

6 Open the lined front bodice out as far as the stitching done in step 4, so that both the lining and the outer bodice are right side up on your work surface. Open out the back bodice in the same way, then lay it right side down on top of the front bodice, aligning the short edges and ensuring that the join at the underarm meets neatly; the ties will be sandwiched in between. Pin together. Work a single straight seam along the sides of first the outer bodice and then the lining. Repeat on the other side of the bodice. Now turn the bodice right side out.

7 Turn under, press, and pin a double ⅜-in. (1-cm) hem along the bottom edge of the skirt fabric. Select a longer stitch (⅛ in./3 mm) on your sewing machine and topstitch along the hem ¼ in. (5 mm) from the edge. Work two rows of gathering stitches (see page 122) within the seam allowance along the top (unhemmed) edge of the skirt. Carefully draw up the threads to gather the fabric until the upper edge of the skirt matches the circumference of the bodice. Knot the gathering threads to secure.

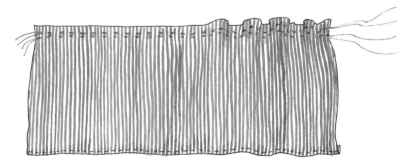

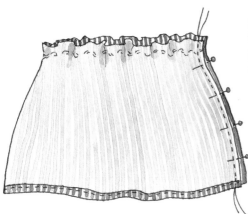

8 Set your stitch length back to normal. With right sides together and aligning the two short edges, fold the skirt in half. Pin in place and machine stitch to form the center back seam. Press the seam open.

✂ **TIP** *Gathering stitch can be worked by hand or with a sewing machine set to a really long stitch length (see page 122); the thread ends are pulled to draw the fabric up to create the gathers.*

9 Pull the bodice lining out slightly, so that it doesn't get caught in the waist seam. With right sides together, slide the skirt over the outer bodice, making sure that the center back seam of the skirt is positioned at the center of the back outer bodice, and pin together. Stitch around the waistline of the skirt to attach it to the outer bodice; the gathering stitches will be concealed within the seam allowance. Press the seam allowances up toward the bodice and turn the dress right side out.

10 Push the lining back into the bodice. Along the bottom edge of the lining, press under about ¼ in. (5 mm) to the wrong side and then slipstitch this to the inside of the skirt to conceal the gathered waist seam allowances.

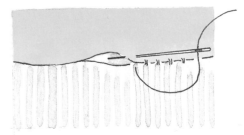

finishing Snip away all remaining thread ends and press to neaten. Tie the straps in neat knots over the shoulders.

classic dungarees

Dungarees or coveralls are a staple for a toddler's closet: they are roomy enough for even the most active toddler and look super cute, too!

YOU WILL NEED

- 60 in. (150 cm) chambray or lightweight denim, 45 in. (115 cm) wide
- 20 in. (50 cm) solid fabric, 45 in. (115 cm) wide
- 2 buttons
- Coordinating thread
- Sewing machine
- Iron
- Dressmaking scissors
- Pins
- Hand sewing needle

SIZES

The patterns are for ages 1–2, 2–3, and 3–4 years.

PATTERN NOTE

Take a ⅜-in. (1-cm) seam allowance throughout, unless otherwise stated.

PATTERN PIECES REQUIRED

Front

Back

Front facing

Back facing

Pocket

Straps

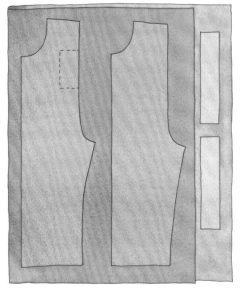

1 Fold one edge of the chambray fabric toward the other long edge, as shown. Cut two fronts and two backs from the folded section, and two straps from the unfolded section.

TIP *The markings on the pattern are used to indicate the position of the pocket and buttonholes; you can use a piece of tailor's chalk or work tailor's tacks to mark them on the fabrics.*

2 Fold the solid fabric as shown, and place the front and back facing sections on the fold. Cut out the facing sections, and cut one pocket and two straps from the unfolded section. Transfer the markings from the pattern pieces to the fabric (see page 121). Zig-zag stitch around all the pieces to secure the raw edges. Press each piece.

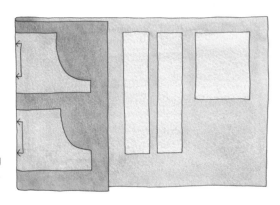

3 Working on each strap in turn, pin one solid cotton and one chambray strap right sides together. Stitch down both long sides and along one short edge, leaving the top short edge open. Clip the corners, turn right side out, and press. Repeat to make the second strap and set aside.

MAKE IT YOURS
Embroider a personalized monogram on the pocket front or sew on a fun fabric patch.

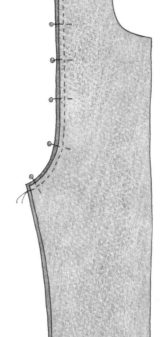

4 Pin the two dungaree fronts right sides together. Working from the top of the bib and ending at the point of the crotch, stitch the center front seam, leaving the inside legs unstitched. Press the seam open. Repeat with the two dungaree back pieces.

5 Along the top edge of the pocket, fold ¼ in. (5 mm) to the wrong side and press. Fold a further ¼ in. (5 mm) to the wrong side, press, and secure with a line of topstitching. Fold ¼ in. (5 mm) to the wrong side along both side edges and the base of the pocket and press. Using the pattern markings as a guide, pin the pocket to the front of the dungaree bib. Topstitch in place around the sides and base.

6 With right sides together, pin the front facing to the dungaree front. Stitch from the bottom of the armhole curve, around the neckline, and down to the second armhole curve, leaving the two side seams unstitched. Clip the seams, turn right side out, and press to neaten.

7 With the chambray side of the straps facing the right side of the back, place the two straps on the dungaree back ⅝ in. (1.5 cm) in from the sides, with the raw edges of the straps extending beyond the top of the dungarees by ⅜ in. (1 cm). Pin and sew in place, stitching within the seam allowance.

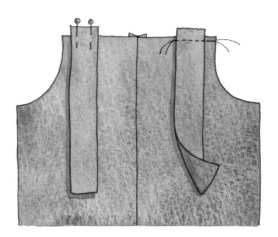

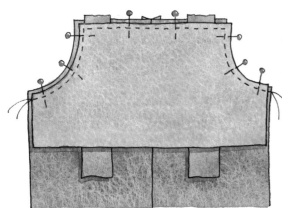

8 With right sides together, pin the back facing to the dungaree back, making sure that the straps are sandwiched between. Stitch together, as in step 6. Clip the seams, turn right side out, and press to neaten.

9 With right sides together, pin the dungaree front and back together and sew the inside leg seam in one continuous seam, leaving the bottom 3 in. (8 cm) unstitched on each leg at the hem edge. Flip the unstitched sections of the facings up, then pin and stitch the side seams, again leaving the bottom 3 in. (8 cm) unstitched. Press the seams open and turn the garment right side out. Press to neaten.

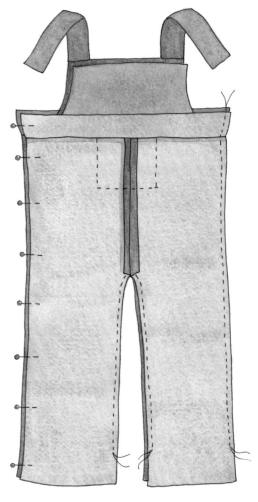

10 Aligning the raw edges and with wrong sides together, stitch the unstitched sections at the bottom of the legs. Turn up 1½ in. (4 cm) and press, then turn up another 1½ in. (4 cm) and press again to make the turn-ups. Hand stitch the turn-ups to the garment at the side seams to secure them in place, if you wish.

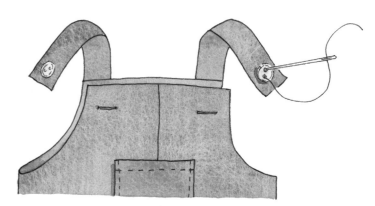

11 Using the pattern markings as a guide, work two buttonholes on the front of the bib section. Sew two buttons onto the straps at the corresponding positions to finish.

finishing Snip away all remaining thread ends and press to neaten.

> **TIP** *You can assess the position of the buttons by slipping the dungarees onto the child and marking where they need to go; this is also great if you need to increase the length slightly as they grow.*

gathered skirt

This slip-on skirt is one of the quickest and easiest garments to make—and there are plenty of options for customizing it with pockets and trims. Pom-pom trim is widely available through craft stores and comes in a range of different colors and sizes. Here, it's stitched into the hem along with the contrast panel and adds a fun feature to the skirt.

YOU WILL NEED

- 20–40 in. (50–100 cm) main fabric the (length depends on the child's measurements), 45 in. (115 cm) wide
- 10 in. (25 cm) contrast fabric, 45 in. (115 cm) wide
- 20–40 in. (50–100 cm) pom-pom trim
- 16 in. (40 cm) elastic, 1 in. (2.5 cm) wide—or 2 in. (5 cm) larger than child's waist measurement
- Coordinating thread
- Sewing machine
- Iron
- Dressmaking scissors
- Pins
- Hand sewing needle
- Safety pin

SIZE

The pattern is created from the child's measurements, so you can fit the skirt to the recipient.

PATTERN NOTE

Take a ⅜-in. (1-cm) seam allowance throughout, unless otherwise stated.

TEMPLATE REQUIRED

Patch pocket template on page 125

1 Measure around the child's waist and multiply by 2 to get the width of the fabric you need. Then measure from the waist to just above the child's knees and add 2 in. (5 cm). Cut one piece to this size from your main fabric. From the contrast fabric, cut one piece the same width as the main fabric piece and 5 in. (13 cm) deep.

MAKE IT YOURS

This simple gathered skirt can be embellished and customized in a number of different ways: here a patch pocket and pom-pom trim have been added, but you could also add a ruffle to the hem or edge it with a length of rick-rack braid.

2 Zig-zag stitch all around the pieces to secure the raw edges. Press each piece.

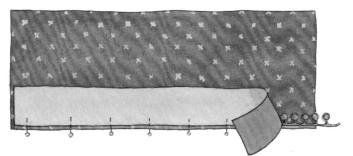

3 Lay the main skirt fabric right side up on your work surface and place a length of pom-pom trim along the long bottom edge, aligning the upper edge of the trim's tape with the raw edge of the fabric. Pin the contrast fabric right side down on top, sandwiching the pom-pom trim between the two layers.

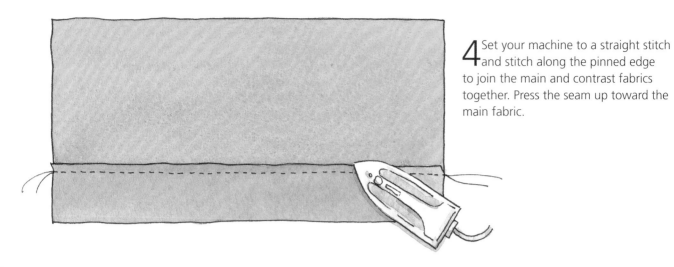

4 Set your machine to a straight stitch and stitch along the pinned edge to join the main and contrast fabrics together. Press the seam up toward the main fabric.

5 Select a longer stitch (⅛ in./3 mm) on your sewing machine and topstitch along the bottom edge of the main fabric, ¼ in. (5 mm) from the seam, to hold the pressed-up seam allowance in place.

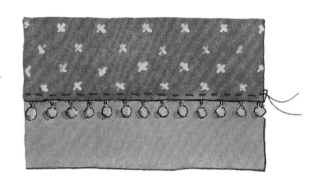

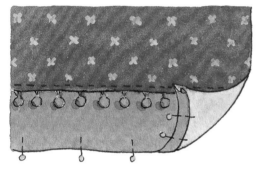

6 Turn under a double ⅜-in. (1-cm) hem along the bottom edge of the contrast fabric, press, and pin in place. With your stitch length still set to ⅛ in. (3 mm), topstitch along the hem to secure, stitching ¼ in. (5 mm) from the edge.

7 To create the center back seam, fold the fabric in half widthwise, right sides together, and pin. For a really neat finish, make sure that the pom-pom seams are aligned. Set your stitch length back to normal. Stitch, then press the seam open.

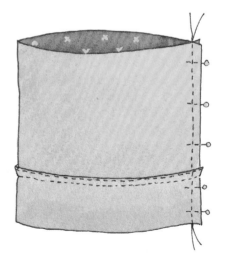

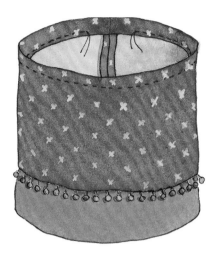

8 Along the top edge of the skirt, fold over ⅜ in. (1 cm) to the wrong side and press. Fold over a further 1½ in. (4 cm), press, and pin in place. Stitch around the waist, working ¼ in. (5 mm) from the folded edge and leaving 1–2 in. (2–5 cm) unstitched at the center back.

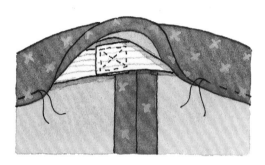

9 Attach the safety pin to one end of the elastic and feed it through the casing at the waistline. Once the elastic is fed through, pull both ends out of the casing and overlap by 1 in. (2.5 cm) to accommodate the child's waist measurement. Carefully box stitch (see page 124) the overlapped ends together, then allow the elastic to slip back inside the casing. Slipstitch the gap in the casing closed.

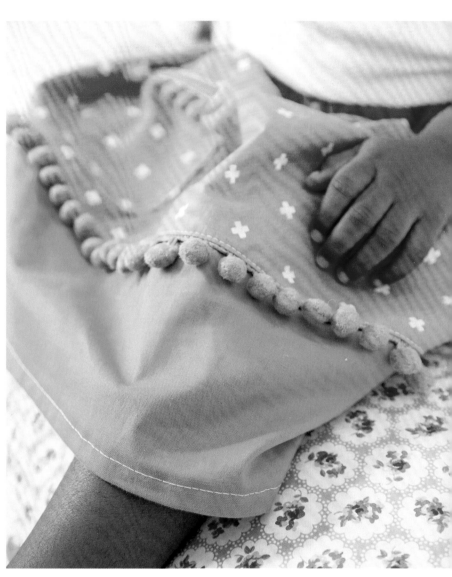

10 Make a paper pattern for the patch pocket, using the template on page 125. Pin the pattern to a small piece of either the main or the contrast fabric and cut it out. Transfer the marks indicating the start and end of the gathering stitches to the fabric (see page 121). Work a line of gathering stitches (see page 122) around the base of the pocket, between the marks, then carefully draw up the threads to curve the base of the pocket. Press under ⅜ in. (1 cm) to the wrong side around the pocket sides and base and pin to secure.

11 Cut a piece of pom-pom trim the same length as the upper edge of the pocket. Cut a piece of contrast fabric 1½ in. (4 cm) deep and the length of the top edge of the pocket plus ⅜ in. (1 cm). Fold and press it in the same way as you would when making bias binding (see page 123). Select a longer stitch (⅛ in./3 mm) on your sewing machine. Align the pom-pom trim tape with the top edge of the pocket, slip the "binding" over the top, pin, and topstitch it in place, stitching ¼ in. (5 mm) from the folded edge.

12 Pin the pocket to the front of the skirt in the desired position. Topstitch around the curved sides and base of the pocket, stitching ¼ in. (5 mm) from the edge.

finishing Snip away all remaining thread ends and press to neaten.

apron pinafore dress

This simple slip-over dress is cleverly constructed with open and overlapping back sections, which means that no fussy fastenings are required. It is also reversible, so it can be simply turned through to the other side for a completely new look.

YOU WILL NEED

- 36 in. (90 cm) lightweight denim, 55 in. (140 cm) wide
- 36 in. (90 cm) print cotton, 54 in. (137 cm) wide
- 5½ yd (5 m) bias binding, 1 in. (2.5 cm) wide (see page 123)
- Coordinating thread
- Sewing machine
- Iron
- Dressmaking scissors
- Pins
- Hand sewing needle

SIZES

The patterns are for ages 2–3, 3–4, and 4–5 years.

PATTERN NOTE

Take a ⅜-in. (1-cm) seam allowance throughout, unless otherwise stated.

PATTERN PIECES REQUIRED

Front
Back
Pocket

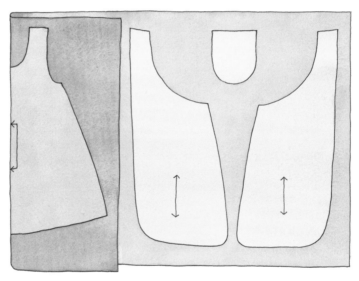

1 Fold one side edge of both the denim and the print cotton fabric in toward the center far enough to accommodate the front piece. From each fabric, cut one front piece on the fold, and one pocket piece and two back pieces on a single layer; remember to flip the pattern piece over when you cut the second back, so that you have a left and a right back. Transfer the markings from the pattern pieces to the fabric (see page 121). Zig-zag stitch around all the pieces to secure the raw edges. Press each piece.

MAKE IT YOURS
Create more of a contrast by using a different cotton fabric for the back pieces on each side.

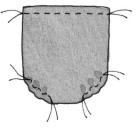 

2 Working on each pocket in turn, work a line of gathering stitches (see page 122) between the marked sections and draw the thread up to create the curved lower section. Along the top edge, press ¼ in. (5 mm) to the wrong side and topstitch it in place. Turn ¼ in. (5 mm) to the wrong side along the sides and the lower section and press.

TIP *The binding is sewn on in one long consecutive seam. As this seam is rather long, try basting (tacking) it in place first before machine stitching and then finishing with hand slipstitches.*

3 Following the pattern markings for placement, pin the denim pocket to the print cotton dress front and the print pocket to the denim dress front. Stitch in place.

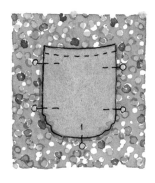 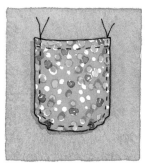

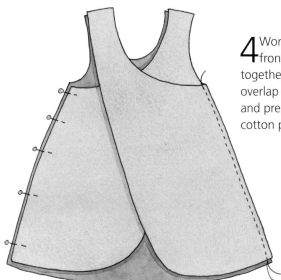

4 Working on the denim pieces first, pin the dress front and the two dress back pieces right sides together along the side seams; there will be an overlap along the center back. Stitch the side seams and press the seams open. Repeat with the print cotton pieces.

TIP *Pressing the garment at each stage will help bring each section together neatly.*

5 Place the denim and the print cotton dresses wrong sides together, aligning the side seams and the raw edges. Take the left back strap and the right front strap of the denim, place them right sides together, and stitch across the short top edge. Repeat with the right back strap and the left front strap of the denim. Fold the denim straps out of the way so that you don't accidentally catch them in the stitching, then stitch the print cotton straps in the same way. Press the shoulder seams open and align the shoulder seams on the print and denim sides.

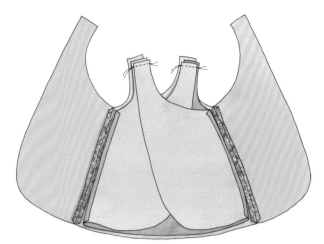

6 With wrong sides together and aligning the strap and side seams, pin the fabrics together and treat as one reversible piece. Work a line of basting (tacking) stitches by hand or machine all around, keeping within the seam allowance, to hold the two layers together.

TIP *Use the tip of the iron to press the binding to ease it around the curves when securing it.*

7 Open out the bias binding. With right sides together and aligning the raw edges, pin, baste, and stitch it to the right side of the print cotton in one continuous strip, working it carefully around the curves and at the base, armholes, and neckline and ending at the center back.

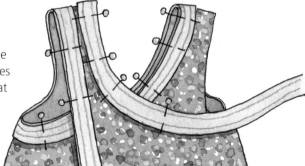

8 Turn the dress through to the other side and fold the binding over. Press to neaten and pin in place to conceal the raw edges. Slipstitch the binding to the other side of the dress to finish.

finishing Snip away all remaining thread ends and press to neaten.

bowling shirt

Combine bold prints with solid shades to give this classic garment a fun twist. The addition of the patch pocket and snap fasteners give a more relaxed feel.

YOU WILL NEED

- 40 in. (1 m) solid fabric, 44 in. (112 cm) wide
- 28 in. (70 cm) patterned fabric, 44 in. (112 cm) wide
- 12-in. (30-cm) square of mediumweight iron-on interfacing
- 5 snap fasteners
- Coordinating thread
- Sewing machine
- Iron
- Dressmaking scissors
- Pins
- Hand sewing needle

SIZES

The patterns are for ages 2–3, 3–4, and 4–5 years.

PATTERN NOTE

Take a ⅜-in. (1-cm) seam allowance throughout, unless otherwise stated.

PATTERN PIECES REQUIRED

Front
Sleeve
Collar
Back
Pocket

1 Fold the solid fabric in half widthwise, from selvage to selvage. Fold one selvage of the patterned fabric in toward the center, just far enough to accommodate the back pattern piece. From the solid fabric, cut two shirt fronts, two sleeves, and two collars. From the patterned fabric, cut one back piece on the fold and one pocket piece on a single layer. Transfer all pattern markings to the fabric (see page 121). Zig-zag stitch around all the pieces to secure the raw edges. Press each piece.

TIP *Placing the pocket piece on a specific area to isolate a motif before cutting in the print—called fussy cutting—will create a striking-looking pocket.*

MAKE IT YOURS

For a more formal style, make the shirt in a single solid-colored cotton and switch out the snaps for traditional shirt buttons and buttonholes.

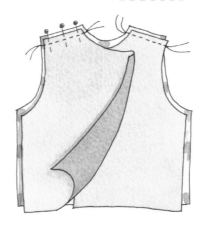

2 With right sides together, pin the front pieces to the back at the shoulder seams. Machine stitch and then press the seams open.

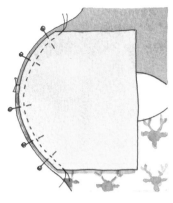

3 Open out the joined front and back pieces and lay the garment flat on your work surface. With right sides together, center the sleeve head (the curved edge of the sleeve) over the armhole and pin and stitch in place. Repeat for the second sleeve. Press the seams toward the arms.

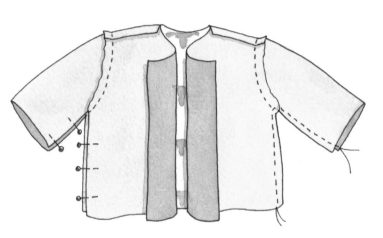

4 Fold the shirt so that the front and back are right sides together, aligning the side and underarm seams, and pin in place. Stitch each side seam in turn, working from the base of the shirt, up the side, and then down the arm, ending at the cuff. Press the seams open.

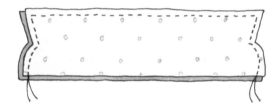

5 Following the manufacturer's instructions, apply iron-on interfacing to the wrong side of one of the collar pieces. Pin the two collar pieces right sides together and stitch around three sides, leaving the neckline edge (the collar stand) unstitched. Trim the points off the seam allowance, turn right side out, and press to neaten.

TIP *Adding interfacing to the collar will help to give the garment a little more structure. Make sure you use a mediumweight interfacing in this project.*

6 Turn the shirt right side out. Align the raw edges of the collar with the neckline edge of the shirt and pin and stitch in place.

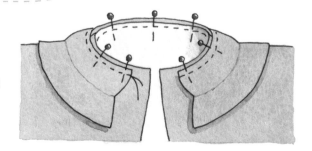

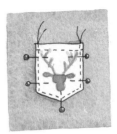

7 Working on each side of the front in turn, fold to the wrong side by ¼ in. (5 mm) and press, then fold a further 1 in. (2.5 cm) to the wrong side and press again to create a placket. Make sure that the ends of the collar stand are neatly tucked within the upper section of the placket. Secure with a line of topstitching, working up one side of the placket ⅛–¼ in. (3–5 mm) from the edge, then across the top to secure the collar, and back down the other side. Repeat to form a placket on the opposite side.

8 Along the top edge of the pocket, press ¼ in. (5 mm) to the wrong side. Secure with a line of topstitching. Fold ¼ in. (5 mm) to the wrong side along both sides and the base and press. Using the pattern markings as a guide, pin the pocket to the front of the shirt. Topstitch in place.

9 Turn under, press, and pin a double ¼-in. (5-mm) hem (see page 121) around the bottom edge of the shirt. Stitch in place.

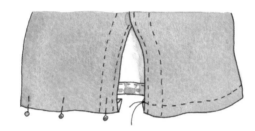

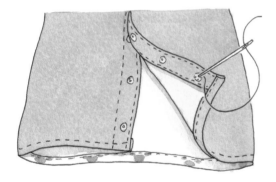

10 Using the pattern markings as a guide, attach five snap fasteners to the front placket, then attach the second part of the snaps to the second placket to correspond. Remember: For a little boy, the left placket (as worn) should overlap the right. Reverse this if you're making the shirt for a little girl.

finishing Snip away all remaining thread ends and press to neaten.

YOU WILL NEED

- 20 in. (50 cm) print cotton, 45 in. (115 cm) wide
- 10 in. (25 cm) contrast fabric, 45 in. (115 cm) wide
- 16 in. (40 cm) elastic, 1 in. (2.5 cm) wide
- Coordinating thread
- Sewing machine
- Iron
- Dressmaking scissors
- Pins
- Safety pin
- Hand sewing needle

SIZES

The patterns are for ages 2–3, 3–4, and 4–5 years.

PATTERN NOTES

For fabrics with larger prints, you may need to increase the fabrics amount to accommodate the motifs and to allow for matching prints where required.

Take a ⅜-in. (1-cm) seam allowance throughout, unless otherwise stated.

PATTERN PIECES REQUIRED

Front
Back
Cuff
Waistband

shorts

As the weather gets warmer, it's the perfect time to get out the shorts. These sweet little elasticated-waist shorts are much easier to put together than you might think! Team a fun print with a solid cotton for the waistband and cuffs to create a striking contrast that will set these apart from store-bought shorts.

1 From the main fabric, cut two front and two back pieces. From the contrast fabric, cut two cuffs and one waistband. Zig-zag stitch around all the pieces to secure the raw edges. Press each piece.

✄ **TIP** *Position the pattern pieces carefully to match the patterns across the seams. Remember to flip the patterns over so you get a left and a right front and back piece.*

2 Pin the two front pieces right sides together, aligning the raw edges. Set your machine to a straight stitch and stitch along the center front seam, working from the top (waist) edge to the bottom of the curve; be sure to leave the lower portion of the piece unstitched, as this will become the inside leg seam. Repeat with the two back pieces. Press the seams open.

3 Aligning the inside legs on each side, pin the back and front pieces right sides together. Starting at the bottom of one leg, stitch up the leg, across the crotch, and back down the other leg. Press the seam open. With the pieces still right sides together, pin and stitch the front and back pieces together along the side seams. Press the seams open. Turn the shorts right side out.

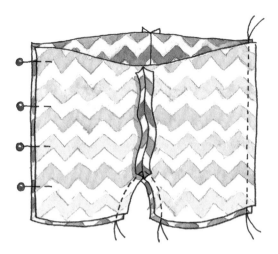

4 With right sides together and aligning the two short edges, fold the cuff strips in half lengthwise. Pin, then stitch the short edges together to form a loop. Press the seam open. Turn the loop right side out, then fold it in half widthwise, with the seam on the inside. With the shorts right side out and aligning the raw edges and the cuff seams with the inside leg seams, slide the cuffs onto the legs of the shorts and pin in place. If possible, remove the extension part of the machine and work with the free arm. Stitch around the lower part of the legs to secure the cuffs in place.

TIP *Before securing the elastic at the waist, slip the shorts onto the child to check the fit.*

5 Fold the seam allowances of the cuffs up, toward the shorts legs, and press. Select a longer stitch (⅛ in./3 mm) on your sewing machine and topstitch along the bottom of the cuffs, ¼ in. (5 mm) from the edge, to secure.

6 Set your stitch length back to normal. Attach the waistband (see page 124), aligning the seam in the waistband with the center back seam and leaving a 1½ in. (4-cm) gap at the center back. Using the safety pin, insert the elastic, box stitch the ends together (see page 124), then slipstitch the gap in the waistband closed.

finishing Snip away all remaining thread ends and press to neaten.

YOU WILL NEED

- 20 in. (50 cm) solid cotton, 45 in. (112 cm) wide
- 20 in. (50 cm) print cotton, 45 in. (112 cm) wide
- 3 buttons, ¾–1 in. (2–2.5 cm) in diameter
- 12-in. (30-cm) square of lightweight iron-on interfacing
- Coordinating thread
- Sewing machine
- Iron
- Dressmaking scissors
- Pins
- Hand sewing needle

SIZES

The patterns are for ages 1–2, 2–3, and 3–4 years.

PATTERN NOTE

Take a ⅜-in. (1-cm) seam allowance throughout, unless otherwise stated.

PATTERN PIECES REQUIRED

Bodice front
Bodice back
Skirt
Collar

peter pan collar dress

This pretty dress is accented with a sweet Peter Pan collar to give a fun, feminine flourish. The bodice buttons at the back and is finished with a full skirt.

1 Fold both fabrics in half widthwise, aligning the selvages. From the solid cotton, cut two bodice fronts on the fold and four bodice backs (two will be the outer fabric, two will be the lining). From the print cotton, cut one skirt on the fold and four collar pieces. Cut two collars in interfacing. Transfer the pattern markings for the buttonholes to the right back bodice and lining pieces (see page 121).

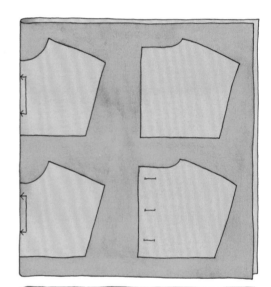

2 Zig-zag stitch around all the fabric pieces to secure the raw edges. Press each piece.

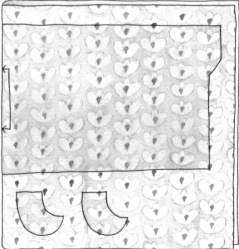

MAKE IT YOURS

Add a length of pretty lace or pom-pom trim to the hem of the skirt.

3 Following the manufacturer's instructions, apply iron-on interfacing to the wrong side of a left and a right collar piece. Place the corresponding collar piece on top, right sides together. Set your machine to a straight stitch and sew along the curved section only. Clip the pointed sections of the seam allowance and snip small V-shapes into the curve. Turn right side out and press to neaten. Topstitch along the curve. Repeat to make the second part of the collar.

TIP *After fusing the interfacing to the collar pieces, leave them on a flat surface to cool; this allows the adhesive of the interfacing to fully bond to the fabric.*

4 Aligning the raw edges of the neckline with the raw edges of the collar, pin the collar pieces to the right side of the outer bodice front and stitch in place, keeping your stitching inside the seam allowance.

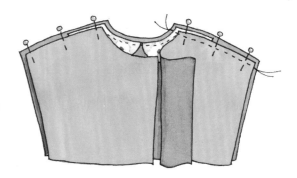

5 With right sides together and aligning the raw edges, pin the front and back outer bodice pieces together at the shoulder seams. The collar ends will be secured in the shoulder seams. Sew the shoulder seams and press the seams open. Repeat with the bodice lining pieces.

6 Open out the outer and lining bodices and pin them right sides together, aligning the raw edges. Starting at the lower hem on one side, working around the neck, and ending at the lower hem on the other side, stitch the outer and lining bodices together at the back opening. The collar will be sandwiched in between. Snip small V-shapes out of the curve to encourage it to lie flat.

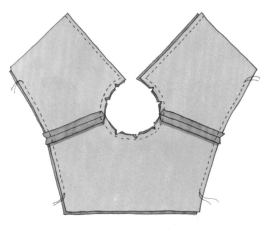

7 Now stitch the side seams, leaving 1¾ in. (4.5 cm) at the ends of each seam unstitched.

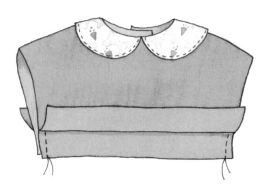

8 Turn the garment right side out and align the raw edges. Fold the outer bodice front and back sections out of the way; with right sides together, complete the side seams on the bodice lining.

9 Turn the garment lining side out. With the completed lining folded away from the stitching line, and with the outer bodice front and back right sides together, stitch the side seams of the outer bodice. This allows the seamed section that sits under the armhholes to have no visilbe raw edges. Turn the garment right side out again and press.

10 With right sides together and aligning the angled section that will form the back skirt placket, fold the skirt in half widthwise and pin the center back seam. Stitch, working around the placket and down to the hem. Press the placket to one side and press the seam open.

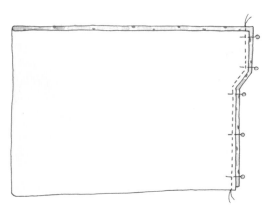

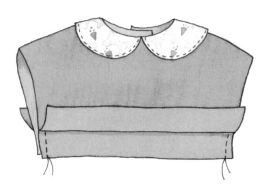

11 Work two lines of gathering stitches (see page 122), either by hand or by machine, along the top edge of the skirt within the seam allowance. Draw up the threads to gather the skirt to the circumference of the bodice, and knot the threads to secure.

12 Pull the bodice lining up out of the way of the stitching line. With right sides together, slide the bodice into the skirt, with the placket section of the skirt along the opening at the center back of the bodice, and pin in place; the placket should be inserted into the right-hand back bodice section (the side where the buttonholes will be stitched) and the remaining skirt into the other side of the bodice. Stitch around the top edge of the skirt to join the skirt and the outer fabric bodice together.

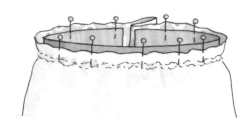

13 Hem the skirt with a double-turned ¼-in. (5-mm) hem (see page 121).

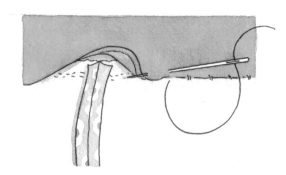

14 Press ¼ in. (5 mm) of the bodice lining to the wrong side and slipstitch it over the seam allowance between the bodice and the skirt.

TIP *Many machines have an automatic buttonhole function to make light work of buttonholes; alternatively you can replace the buttons with snap fasteners.*

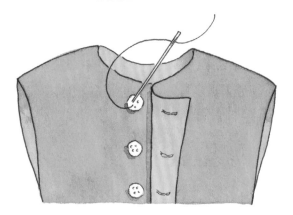

15 Following the pattern markings, work three buttonholes on the right-hand back bodice. Sew the buttons onto the left-hand side to correspond.

finishing Snip away all remaining thread ends and press to neaten.

snuggly pjs with kimono-style top

Get your little ones all ready for dreamland with a pair of comfy pajamas with a kimono-style wrap top. Made from ultra-cozy brushed cotton, they're just the thing for snuggling up on winter evenings.

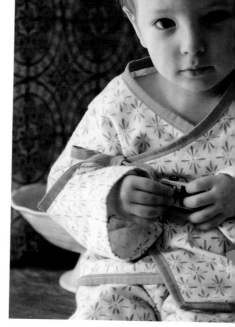

YOU WILL NEED

- 2 yd (1.8 m) brushed cotton, 45 in. (115 cm) wide
- 20 in. (50 cm) elastic, ¾ in. (2 cm) wide
- 3⅞ yd (3.5 m) bias binding, 1 in. (2.5 cm) wide
- Sewing machine
- Iron
- Dressmaking scissors
- Pins
- Safety pin
- Hand sewing needle

SIZES

The patterns are for ages 2–3, 3–4, and 4–5 years.

PATTERN NOTE

Take a ⅜-in. (1-cm) seam allowance throughout, unless otherwise stated.

PATTERN PIECES REQUIRED

Pants front
Pants back
Wrap-top front
Wrap-top back
Sleeve

CUT OUT ALL THE PIECES

1 As you're making a matching set, lay out and cut all the pieces for the pants and top at the same time. Fold the fabric in half widthwise, aligning the selvages. Cut one wrap-top back on the fold and two wrap-top fronts, two sleeves, two pants fronts, and two pants backs. Transfer the pattern markings to the fabric (see page 121). Zig-zag stitch around all the pieces to secure the raw edges. Press each piece.

TIP *Brushed cotton and flannel fabrics can shrink considerably, so it's a good idea to pre-wash and press these materials before you cut out the pattern pieces.*

PANTS

1 Pin the pants front pieces right sides together. Set your machine to a straight stitch and stitch the center front seam, working from the top (waist) edge to the bottom of the curve; leave the lower portion of the piece unstitched, as this will become the inside leg seam. Stitch the back pieces together in the same way. Press the seams open.

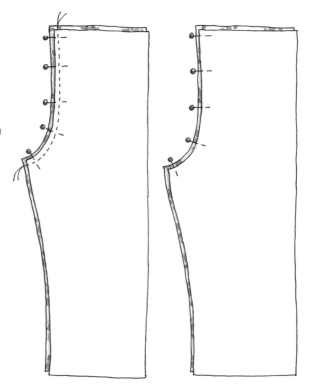

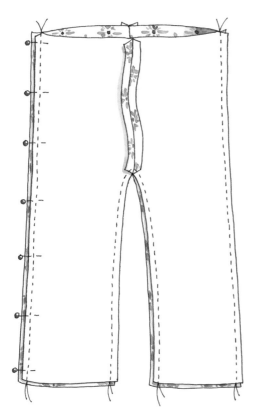

2 Aligning the inside legs on each side, pin the back and front pieces right sides together. Starting at the bottom of one leg, stitch up the leg, across the crotch, and back down the other leg. Press the seam open. Then stitch the side seams and press the seams open.

3 Along the top edge of the pants, fold over ⅜ in. (1 cm) to the wrong side and press. Fold over a further 1½ in. (4 cm), press, and pin in place. Stitch around the waist, working ¼ in. (5 mm) from the folded edge and leaving 2 in. (5 cm) unstitched at the center back. Attach the safety pin to one end of the elastic, feed it through the casing at the waistline, and overlap the ends by about 1 in. (2.5 cm). Carefully box stitch (see page 124) the overlapped ends together, then allow the elastic to slip back inside the casing. Slipstitch the gap in the casing closed.

4 Hem the legs with a double-turned ⅜-in. (1-cm) hem (see page 121).

WRAP TOP

1 With right sides together, pin the front pieces to the back at the shoulder seams. Machine stitch and then press the seams open.

MAKE IT YOURS

For a summery version, create this set in a light, fresh cotton. Reduce the length of the trousers to create cute sleep shorts.

2 Cut two 12-in. (30-cm) lengths of bias binding for the ties. Fold under one short end of each piece, then fold each length in half widthwise and press. Topstitch down the length of the folded edges and across the tucked-in short edge. Using the markings on the pattern as a guide, pin the ties to the armholes of the front pieces, one on the right side and one on the wrong side of the fabric as shown, aligning the raw edges.

3 Open out the joined front and back and lay the garment flat on your work surface. With right sides together, pin the sleeve head (the curved edge of the sleeve) over the armhole and stitch in place. The ties will be secured in the seam. Repeat for the second sleeve. Press the seams open.

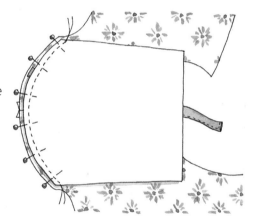

4 Fold the top so that the front and back are right sides together, aligning the side and underarm seams, and pin in place. Stitch each side seam in turn, working from the base of the shirt, up the side, and then down the arm, ending at the cuff. Press the seams open.

5 Hem the sleeves with a double-turned ⅜-in. (1-cm) hem (see page 121).

(see page 121)

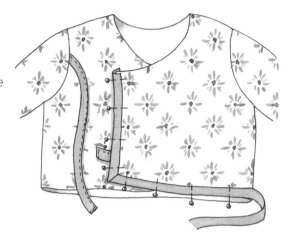

TIP *Mitering the binding on the corners at the base of the top creates a neat finish.*

6 With the top right side up, place the binding over the raw edges at the top of one front section and pin in place, pinning down the one side of the front, around the bottom edge, and back to the top of the opposite front, mitering at the bottom corners. Trim away the excess binding and set aside. Topstitch in place.

7 Pin the remaining binding around the neckline, ensuring that 12 in. (30 cm) of binding extends at each end to create the other parts of the ties. Tuck the raw edges of the ties inside before stitching, and topstitch in place.

finishing Snip away all remaining thread ends and press to neaten. Fold one side of the top in and secure the tie on the inside with a small bow, then fold the second side over and secure with a bow.

CHAPTER 3

accessories

Stitched accessories are not only super cute, but also really useful to have on hand for keeping baby occupied or clean and tidy when out and about. These accessories are great mini makes that are perfect projects for working on while your little one naps.

YOU WILL NEED

- 8 x 22½ in. (20 x 57 cm) solid pink cotton fabric
- 16 x 24 in. (40 x 60 cm) oilcloth
- 17½ x 25½ in. (44 x 64 cm) white toweling
- 16 x 24 in. (40 x 60 cm) quilt batting (wadding)
- 4 snap fasteners
- Coordinating thread
- Sewing machine
- Teflon foot
- Iron
- Dressmaking scissors
- Pins

SIZE

16 x 20 in. (40 x 60 cm)

PATTERN NOTE

Take a ⅜-in. (1-cm) seam allowance throughout, unless otherwise stated.

PATTERN PIECES REQUIRED

None

on-the-go changing mat

Keep baby clean and fresh with this easy-make changing mat, which uses both ultra-soft toweling and wipe-clean oilcloth to give two changing surfaces that will allow you to deal with whatever life throws at you! The mat can be folded up and secured with snap fasteners, so you can stow it away in your diaper (nappy) bag or attach it to your stroller.

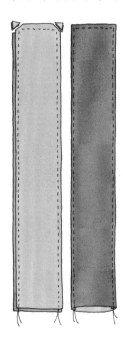

1 Cut the pink cotton into two 4 x 22½-in. (10 x 57-cm) strips and pin them right sides together. Stitch together along one short edge and both long edges, leaving one short edge unstitched. Snip off the corners, turn right side out, and press. Select a longer stitch (⅛ in./ 3 mm) on your sewing machine and topstitch around the three seamed edges of the pink strip, ¼ in. (5 mm) from the edge.

TIP *To make a larger changing mat simply increase the fabric amounts, ensuring that there is an additional ¾ in. (2 cm) of toweling backing all around.*

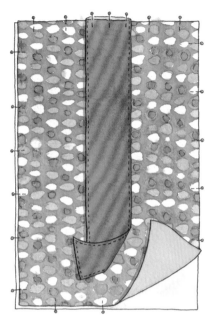

2 Place the oilcloth right side up on top of the batting (wadding). Place the unstitched edge of the pink strip in the center of one of the short edges of the oilcloth, aligning the raw edges, and pin in place. Attach a Teflon foot to your machine and set your stitch length back to normal. Stitch all around, stitching through all layers, to secure the pink strip in place.

3 With wrong sides together, center the oilcloth on top of the toweling, leaving an even ¾-in. (2-cm) border of toweling all around. Fold the toweling over the oilcloth, tuck under the raw edges, and pin in place. Neatly miter the corners (see page 119) and pin to secure. Select a longer stitch (⅛ in./3 mm) on your sewing machine. Holding the pink strip away from the stitching lines, topstitch around the mat ¼ in. (5 mm) from the folded edge of the toweling.

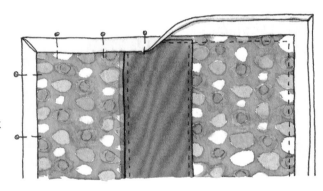

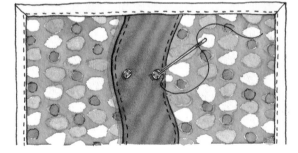

4 Lay the pink strip down the center of the mat. Stitch one half of two snap fasteners 2¾ in. (7 cm) down from the edge that's caught under the toweling backing, positioning one on each side of the pink strip.

✄ **TIP** *If you don't have a Teflon foot, which is designed to glide over fabrics such as oilcloth, you can prevent your standard foot from getting stuck by placing a piece of baking parchment on top of the oilcloth before you stitch. The foot will glide easily over the baking parchment and you can carefully rip off the paper once the seams have been stitched.*

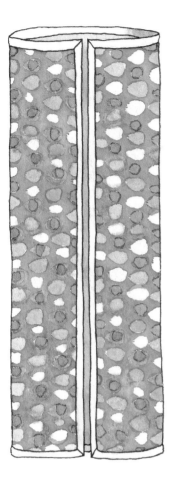

5 With the toweling side uppermost, fold the two long side edges in toward the center. Fold the bottom edge up by one-third, then fold it up again. Bring the pink strip around the folded mat, then attach the other halves of the snap fasteners to the underside of the pink strip to correspond with the snaps attached in step 4.

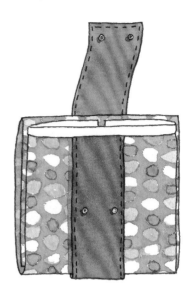

finishing Snip away all remaining thread ends and press to neaten.

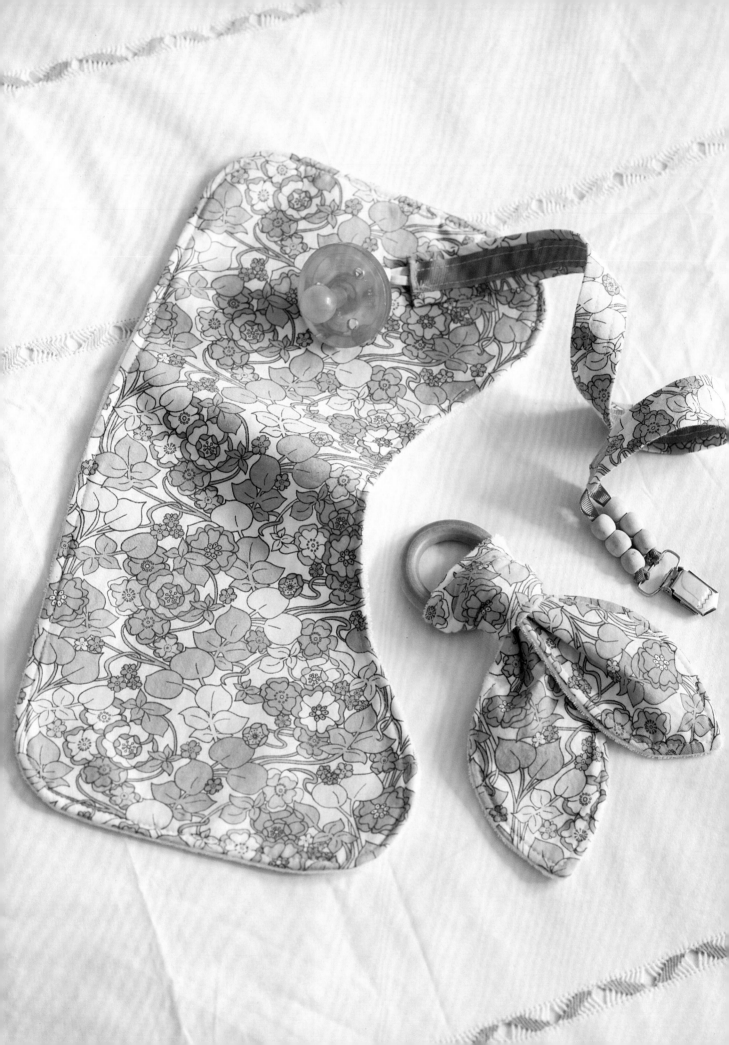

YOU WILL NEED

- 14 x 59 in. (35 x 150 cm) print jersey to make whole set
- 14 x 59 in. (35 x 150 cm) of stretch toweling to make whole set
- 14 x 59 in. (35 x 150 cm) lightweight iron-on stretch interfacing
- 3 in. (8 cm) elastic, ¼ in. (5 mm) wide
- 12 in. (30 cm) ribbon, ⅜ in. (1 cm) wide
- 16 in. (40 cm) ribbon, ⅝ in. (1.5 cm) wide
- Wooden teething ring (available from craft stores or Etsy)
- 6 small wooden beads
- Metal suspender/brace clip
- Sewing machine with a stretch stitch and ballpoint/jersey needle
- Iron
- Dressmaking scissors
- Pins
- Knitting needle

SIZES

Burpie: 8 x 15 in. (20 x 38 cm)
Teether: 6 in. (15 cm), including ring
Pacifier clip: 20 in. (50 cm), including clip

PATTERN NOTES

Ensure that all wooden elements have been treated with child-safe/food-safe wax or treatment.

Take a ⅜-in. (1-cm) seam allowance throughout, unless otherwise stated.

TEMPLATES REQUIRED

Burpie template on page 124
Teether template on page 125

baby gifts bundle

This sweet little set is the ideal gift for a new mother or to pack into your diaper (nappy) bag to take with you on the go. It includes a fabric teether that will keep baby occupied, a pretty pacifier (dummy) clip, and a handy burpie cloth that is contoured to fit mom's shoulder to catch any unwanted mess!

BURPIE AND TEETHER

1 Following the manufacturer's instructions, apply iron-on interfacing to the wrong side of the stretch jersey.

2 Make paper patterns, using the templates on pages 124 and 125. Fold the print jersey and stretch toweling in half. Place the patterns on the fold and cut one from each fabric.

> ✂ **TIP** *Applying a fusible interfacing with a slight stretch is a great way to give the fabric a little more stability so that it is easier to stitch without losing its shape, but won't change the handle of the fabric too much.*

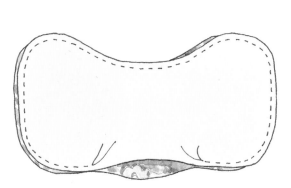

3 Pin the jersey and toweling pieces for the burpie and teether right sides together. Insert a ballpoint needle into your machine and select a stretch stitch. Stitch around the pieces, leaving a 2–3-in. (5–8-cm) gap along the straight edge. Along the curved edges, snip small V-shapes in the seam allowance to ease the curve when turning through, being very careful not to cut through the stitching. Snip off the points of the teether.

> **MAKE IT YOURS**
> This set can easily be made from leftover jersey fabric from your stash or an upcycled T-shirt. Be sure to check the remnant selection at your local fabric store for pretty bargains.

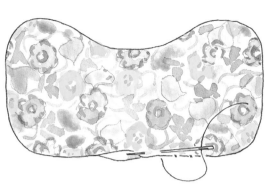

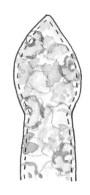

4 Turn the pieces right side out, using a knitting needle to push out the curved and pointed sections. Carefully push the seam allowances along the gaps to the inside, press to neaten, and pin in place. Slipstitch the gaps closed. Select a longer stitch (⅛ in./3 mm) on your sewing machine and topstitch around the outer edge, ¼ in. (5 mm) from the edge.

TIP *These makes use only small amounts of fabric, so you can mix and match prints from your stash. Experiment with the placement of the templates to position any motifs on the finished make; this technique is called "fussy cutting."*

FOR THE TEETHER ONLY

5 Fold the fabric teether in half, placing the two pointed ends on top on each other to form a loop. Feed it through the wooden teething ring, draw the ends through the loop, and pull tight to anchor it onto the ring.

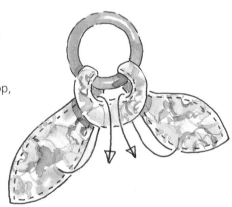

finishing Snip away all remaining thread ends and press to neaten.

PACIFIER CLIP

1 From the remaining jersey fabric, cut a piece measuring 2 x 16 in. (5 x 40 cm). Fold under ⅜ in. (1 cm) at each short end and press. Press each long side in to the center.

2 Fold the length of elastic in half, place the cut ends inside the folded section at one short end of the jersey strip, and pin in place.

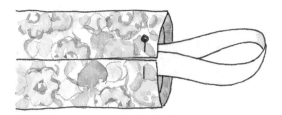

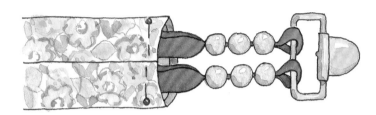

3 Cut the narrower of the two ribbons into two 6-in. (15-cm) lengths. Thread three wooden beads onto one end of each ribbon. Secure the metal suspender/brace clip at the center of the two ribbons, then knot each ribbon to secure. Slide the ribbon into the center of the jersey strip at the opposite end to the elastic and pin it in place.

4 Place the wider ribbon down the center of the folded jersey strip, concealing the raw edges and allowing ⅜ in. (1 cm) to overhang at each end, and pin in place. Carefully tuck the excess ribbon at each end into the folded strip and re-pin to secure.

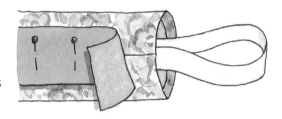

5 Select a longer stitch (⅛ in./ 3mm) on your sewing machine and topstitch around the outer edge of the ribbon, about ⅛ in. (2–3 mm) from the edge.

finishing Snip away all remaining thread ends to neaten. Secure a pacifier (dummy) securely to the loop of elastic.

TIP *For tips on working with stretch and knit fabrics, see pages 109 and 110.*

YOU WILL **NEED**

For the towel

- 60 in. (150 cm) print cotton, 44 in. (112 cm) wide
- 60 in. (150 cm) white toweling, 44 in. (112 cm) wide
- 165 in. (4.2 m) piping cord in contrasting color

For the washcloth

- 10-in. (25-cm) square of print cotton
- 10-in. (25-cm) square of white toweling
- 6 x 1¾-in. (15 x 4.5-cm) print cotton for hanging loop
- 37½ in. (95 cm) piping in contrasting color
- Coordinating thread

- Sewing machine
- Iron
- Dressmaking scissors
- Pins
- Hand sewing needle
- Rotary cutter, ruler, and cutting mat (optional)

SIZES

Hooded towel: 34¾ in. (88 cm) square
Washcloth: 9¼ in. (23 cm) square

PATTERN NOTE

Take a ⅜-in. (1-cm) seam allowance throughout, unless otherwise stated.

PATTERN PIECES REQUIRED

None

hooded bath towel

Keep little ones cozy at bath time with this snuggly towel. Created from soft toweling, it features a small hood on the upper corner which is perfect for drying hair and makes it ideal for swaddling up little ones to dry them before bed. Complete the bath time set with a simple coordinating washcloth.

HOODED TOWEL

1 Using dressmaking scissors—or a rotary cutter, ruler, and mat—cut a triangle measuring 13¾ x 13¾ x 18 in. (25 x 35 x 46 cm) from both the print cotton and the toweling. Cut an 18-in. (46-cm) length of piping.

TIP *Using a rotary cutter, ruler, and mat to cut the fabrics for the hood section will help to create a neat, even triangle.*

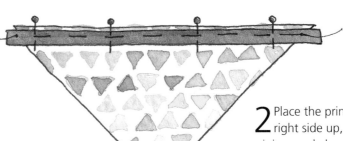

2 Place the print cotton triangle right side up, and pin the piping cord along the longest edge, aligning the raw edges of the fabric and piping tape. Pin in place; you may also wish to hand baste (tack) the piping to make sure it doesn't slip.

MAKE IT YOURS
You can use a large bath towel as a base for this make and team it with your favorite print cotton.

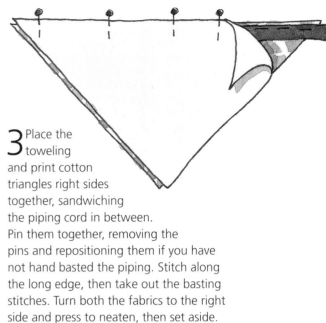

3 Place the toweling and print cotton triangles right sides together, sandwiching the piping cord in between. Pin them together, removing the pins and repositioning them if you have not hand basted the piping. Stitch along the long edge, then take out the basting stitches. Turn both the fabrics to the right side and press to neaten, then set aside.

4 Cut a 35½-in. (90-cm) square from both the print cotton and the toweling. Pin or baste piping cord all around the right side of the print cotton, as in step 2. Where the tape ends meet, overlap them, trim away any excess, and fold inside any raw edges.

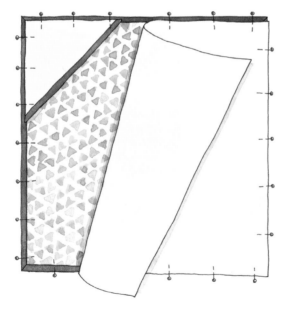

5 Place the print cotton square right side up on your work surface, with the triangle from step 3 on top, toweling side up, aligning the raw edges. Place the toweling square right side down on top of that. Pin all the layers together.

6 Stitch around the outer edge, leaving a 3–4-in. (8–10-cm) gap along one side for turning through. Cut away any excess fabrics along the seam allowances, trim the corners to reduce bulk, and turn right side out through the gap in the seam. Press the seam allowance inside and slipstitch the gap closed.

finishing Snip away all remaining thread ends and press to neaten.

WASHCLOTH

1 Fold and press the contrast strip for the hanging loop in the same way as you would when making bias binding (see page 123). Select a longer stitch (⅛ in./3 mm) on your sewing machine and topstitch ¼ in. (5 mm) from each of the outer folded edges in turn. Set aside.

2 Pin or baste piping cord all around the right side of the print cotton, as in step 2 of the hooded towel. Where the tape ends meet, overlap them, trim away any excess, and fold inside any raw edges.

3 With the print cotton right side up, place the hanging loop across one corner, approximately 3½ in. (9 cm) down from the corners, ensuring that the raw edges of the loop extend slightly beyond the print cotton. Pin in place.

4 With right sides together, position the toweling on top of the print cotton; the hanging loop and piping cord will be sandwiched in between. Pin them together, removing the pins and repositioning them if you have not hand basted the piping. Stitch around the outer edge of the washcloth, leaving a 3-in. (8-cm) gap along one side to turn through.

5 Cut away any excess fabrics along the seam allowances, trim the corners to reduce bulk, and turn right side out through the gap in the seam. Press the seam allowance inside and slipstitch the gap closed.

finishing Snip away all remaining thread ends to neaten.

YOU WILL NEED

For the rabbit toy

- Fat quarter of light brown baby cord
- Scraps of print cotton
- Child-safe toy stuffing
- Brown embroidery floss (thread)

For the bed

- Fat quarter of print cotton
- Fat quarter of white cotton lining
- Fat quarter of quilt batting (wadding)
- Small amount of toy stuffing
- Coordinating thread
- Sewing machine
- Iron
- Dressmaking scissors
- Pins
- Hand sewing needle
- Knitting needle

SIZES

Rabbit: 12½ in. (32 cm) long to tip of ears
Bed: 6¾ x 10¼ in. (17 x 26 cm)

PATTERN NOTE

Take a ⅜-in. (1-cm) seam allowance throughout, unless otherwise stated.

TEMPLATES REQUIRED

Rabbit body
Rabbit arm
Rabbit ear
all on page 126

bring-along bunny and quilted bed

This sweet rabbit toy is cute and quick to make and is sure to become a firm favorite with little ones. Create a mini quilted bed to make this the perfect nap-time toy.

RABBIT TOY

1 Make paper patterns from the templates on page 126. Using the patterns, cut two bodies, four arms, and two ears from the brown baby cord. Also cut two ears from the print cotton.

2 Zig-zag stitch all around each piece to secure the raw edges. Press each piece.

> ✂ **TIP** *A "fat quarter" is a yard or meter of fabric that is folded in half both horizontally and vertically, and then cut into four along the fold lines—so you end up with a piece measuring 18 in. high x 22 in. wide (50 x 56 cm), compared to a normal quarter yard or meter, which measures 44 x 9 in. (112 x 23 cm). Fat quarters are sold in quilting stores.*

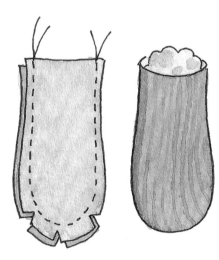

3 Pin two arm pieces right sides together. Set your machine to a straight stitch and stitch around the curved sides, leaving the top (straight) edge open. Snip small V-shapes in the seam allowance to ease the curve when turning through, being very careful not to cut through the stitching. Turn right side out and stuff lightly with toy stuffing. Repeat to make a second arm.

4 Pin one print cotton and one baby cord ear right sides together. Stitch them together in the same way as the arms, snip the seam allowance, and turn right side out. Repeat to make a second ear.

5 Using all six strands of a length of brown embroidery floss (thread), neatly embroider the eyes and nose onto the right side of one of the body pieces, using the photograph as a guide.

TIP *Ensure that all seams are stitched securely and always use child-safe toy stuffing for children's toys.*

6 Place the ears on the head, with the print cotton side facing the embroidered section and aligning the raw edges. Baste (tack) them in place within the seam allowance. Pin and baste the arms to the sides of the body in the same way.

7 Pin the remaining body piece right side down on top of the embellished front part, aligning all the curves and raw edges. Stitch the rabbit front and back together, leaving a gap of about 2 in. (5 cm) on one side unstitched, for turning through.

8 Snip small V-shapes in the seam allowance to ease the curve when turning through, being very careful not to cut through the stitching. Turn right side out, using a knitting needle to ease out the legs.

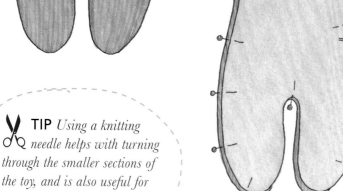

TIP *Using a knitting needle helps with turning through the smaller sections of the toy, and is also useful for pushing in the stuffing.*

MAKE IT YOURS
Adapt the pattern pieces to create your own menagerie of soft plush toys. Why not create a bear, fox, or raccoon?

9 Stuff the rabbit with toy stuffing, working with small pieces at a time and pushing it into all parts of the body, legs, and head. Around the gap, tuck in the seam allowance and slipstitch the gap closed.

QUILTED BED

1 Cut the print cotton to 7½ x 17¾ in. (19 x 45 cm), the white cotton to 7½ x 19 in. (19 x 48 cm), and the batting (wadding) to 7½ x 21 in. (19 x 53 cm).

2 Zig-zag stitch all around the two cotton pieces to secure the raw edges. Press each piece.

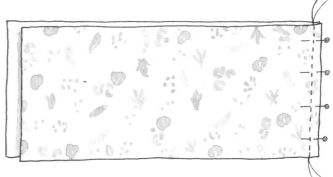

3 Pin the white cotton and print cotton right sides together, aligning one of the short ends. Set your machine to a straight stitch and stitch the pieces together along this edge to make a long strip. Press the seam open.

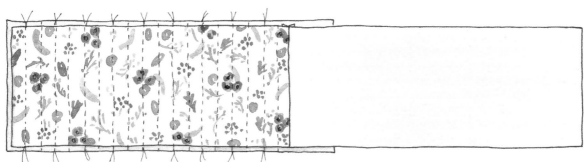

4 Place the print cotton end of the strip right side up on the batting (wadding), aligning them at the short end, and pin together. Stitch a series of quilting lines across the width of the print cotton, spacing them a machine foot's width apart, until you reach the seam with the white cotton.

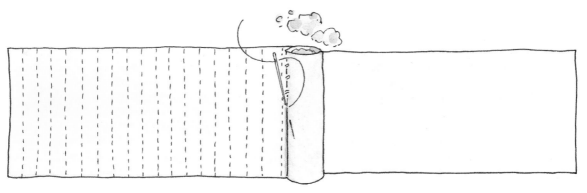

5 Turn the piece over so that the batting side is uppermost. At the seam between the two cotton pieces, fold the batting over by 2½ in. (6 cm) and slipstitch it to the seam line to form a hollow tube. Insert a small amount of stuffing to create a pillow effect.

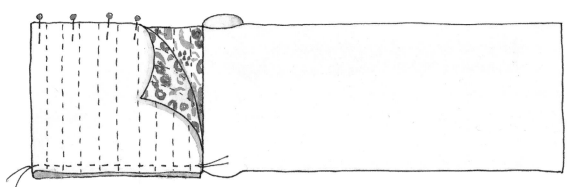

6 Turn the piece over again, so that the print cotton side is uppermost. Fold the quilted print cotton up, right sides together, aligning the raw edge with the base of the pillow section, and pin in place. Stitch the two side seams, snip the points off the corners of the seam allowance, and turn the quilted section right side out.

7 Fold the white lining in half, right sides together, and pin in place. Starting from the fold, stitch the two side seams, leaving the last 1½ in. (4 cm) on each side unstitched. Neatly clip the points off the corners of the seam allowance, turn the lining right side out, and push it into the quilted bed.

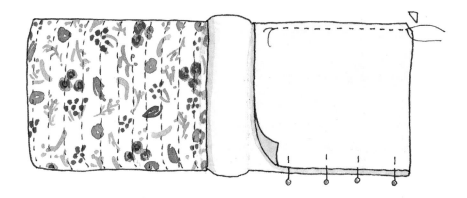

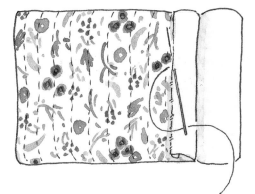

8 Pull the unstitched 1½ in. (4 cm) over to the front of the quilted section and press under ⅜ in. (1 cm) along each side and ⅜ in. (1 cm) along the base. Slipstitch it in place. Turn in the ends of the pillow and slipstitch them together.

finishing Snip away all remaining thread ends and press to neaten.

knotted headband

Worked in soft and stretchy jersey, this neat headband is a great way to tame a little girl's wild hair—and is so comfortable she can wear it all day!

YOU WILL NEED

- 8 x 24 in. (20 x 60 cm) jersey fabric
- 8 x 24 in. (20 x 60 cm) lightweight iron-on stretch interfacing
- Coordinating thread
- Sewing machine with a stretch stitch and ballpoint/jersey needle
- Iron
- Dressmaking scissors
- Pins
- Hand sewing needle
- Knitting needle

SIZE

25 in. (64 cm) long x 1½ in. (4.5 cm) wide, but can be made larger or smaller to fit the child.

PATTERN NOTE

Take a ⅜-in. (1-cm) seam allowance throughout, unless otherwise stated.

TEMPLATE REQUIRED

Headband template on page 126

MAKE IT YOURS
This pattern can be made larger or smaller by simply increasing or reducing the straight center section.

1 Following the manufacturer's instructions, apply lightweight iron-on interfacing to the wrong side of the jersey fabric.

2 Fold the jersey fabric in half, wrong sides together. Make a paper pattern using the template on page 126. Place the pattern on the fold, pin in place, and cut out two pieces. If you are using two separate prints or colors of jersey, cut one piece from each fabric.

✂ **TIP** *Measure around the child's head and compare this to the unshaped part of the pattern piece before cutting; this way you can amend the pattern if necessary for a custom fit.*

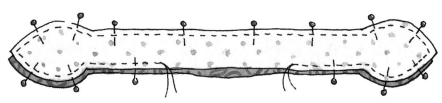

3 Pin the two pieces right sides together, aligning the raw edges. Insert a ballpoint needle into your machine and select a stretch stitch. Stitch all around the headband, pivoting the needle at the points of the ties and leaving a 2-in. (5-cm) gap in the center of one straight edge.

✂ **TIP** *A stretch stitch is a common feature on sewing machines and creates a stitch that has a percentage of movement to accommodate that of stretch fabrics. This helps to prevent the threads from snapping along the seam lines. If you don't have a stretch stitch, select a medium-to-long (around 3.5) straight stitch and experiment with lowering the stitch tension.*

TIP *Ballpoint (jersey) needles are specially created for using with knit fabrics, as they have a rounded tip that is designed to pass neatly through the fibers without damaging or breaking them.*

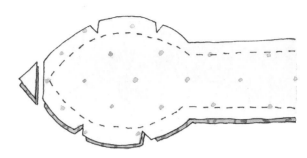

4 Carefully snip off the points at the ends of the ties and trim down any bulky sections of seam allowance. Along the curved sections of the ties, snip small V-shapes in the seam allowance to ease the curve when turning through, being very careful not to cut through the stitching.

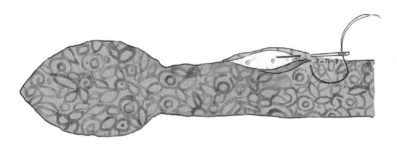

5 Turn the headband right side out through the gap in the stitching, using a knitting needle to push out the points of the ties. Carefully push the seam allowance inside the headband around the gap, press to neaten, and pin in place. Slipstitch the gap closed.

6 Select a longer stitch (⅛ in./3mm) on your sewing machine and topstitch around the headband ¼ in. (5 mm) from the edge, taking care to pivot at the points of the ties.

finishing Snip away all remaining thread ends and press to neaten. Wrap the headband around the child's head and secure the ties in a neat knot.

taggy comfort blanket and drawstring bag

Babies love the tactile feel of ribbon tags, and teamed with the ultra-snuggly textured backing this makes the perfect comfort blanket. Complete with its own mini drawstring bag, it is ready to tote or to gift!

YOU WILL NEED

For the blanket

- 21-in. (52-cm) square of cotton print fabric
- 21-in. (52-cm) square of textured minky or "cuddle" fleece
- Five 20-in. (50-cm) lengths of ribbon in different finishes and colors

For the drawstring bag

- Two 9½ x 10¼-in. (24.5 x 27-cm) pieces of main fabric
- Two 3 x 10-½ in. (8 x 24.5-cm) strips of contrast fabric in a solid color
- Two 2 x 21-in. (5 x 52-cm) strips of fabric or two 21-in. (52-cm) lengths of ribbon for the ties
- Coordinating thread
- Sewing machine
- Iron
- Dressmaking scissors or rotary cutter, cutting mat, and ruler
- Pins
- Hand sewing needle
- Safety pin

SIZES

Blanket: 20 in. (50 cm) square
Drawstring bag: 8½ x 10¾ in. (22.5 x 28 cm)

PATTERN NOTE

Take a ⅜-in. (1-cm) seam allowance throughout unless otherwise stated.

COMFORT BLANKET

1 Zig-zag stitch all around the cotton print and fleece fabrics to secure the raw edges. Press each piece.

2 Cut each of the ribbons into four 4¾ in. (12-cm) lengths, so that you have 20 pieces in total. Fold each ribbon in half. Aligning the raw edges, pin five pieces (one of each ribbon) along each edge of the right side of the cotton print fabric, spacing them evenly. Set your machine to a straight stitch and stitch all around the print fabric ¼ in. (5 mm) from the edge to secure the ribbons in place. Remove the pins.

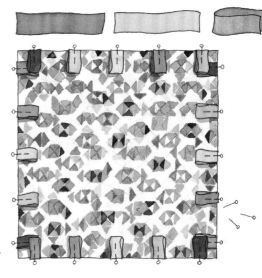

3 With right sides together and aligning the raw edges, pin the fleece backing fabric to the print fabric; the ribbons will be sandwiched in between. Machine stitch around the edge of the fabrics, leaving a 2-in. (5-cm) gap in the center of one side. Snip off the corners to reduce the bulk and trim any bulky seams.

✂ **TIP** *Using a rotary cutter and ruler is a great way to cut very exact straight lines, so it is ideal for items like this that need to be precise.*

MAKE IT YOURS
Add in more ribbons or other tactile elements such as a pom-pom trim to make a more sensory blanket.

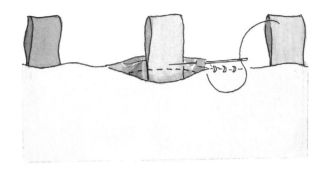

4 Turn the blanket right side out through the gap and use a knitting needle to ease out the four corners. Fold in the seam allowance around the gap in the seam, press, and pin in place. Slipstitch the gap closed.

5 Set your machine to a longer stitch (⅛ in./3 mm) and topstitch around the blanket ¼ in. (5 mm) from the edge, taking care to pivot at the corners.

TIP *Sewing the ribbons in place before stitching the main and backing fabrics together prevents the ribbons from sliding apart and helps to create a neat finish.*

DRAWSTRING BAG

1 Zig-zag stitch all around the main and contrast fabrics to secure the raw edges. Press each piece.

2 Pin the main fabrics right sides together, aligning the raw edges. Set your machine to a straight stitch. Stitch from the upper edge down one long side, across the base, and up the second long side, leaving the top edge unstitched.

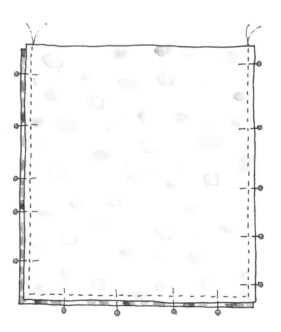

3 On each short end of the solid color strips, fold over ⅜ in. (1 cm) to the wrong side and press. Select a longer stitch (⅛ in./3 mm) on your sewing machine and topstitch across each end ¼ in. (5 mm) from the fold to secure.

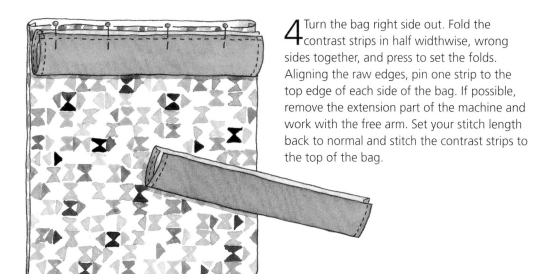

4 Turn the bag right side out. Fold the contrast strips in half widthwise, wrong sides together, and press to set the folds. Aligning the raw edges, pin one strip to the top edge of each side of the bag. If possible, remove the extension part of the machine and work with the free arm. Set your stitch length back to normal and stitch the contrast strips to the top of the bag.

5 Press the contrast strips up and press the seam allowances down, toward the bag. Select a longer stitch (⅛ in./ 3 mm) on your sewing machine and topstitch around the top edge of the main fabric, ¼ in. (5 mm) from the seam.

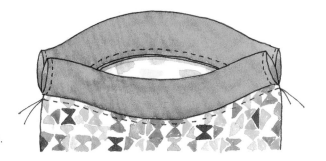

6 If you're making the ties from the contrast fabric, fold and press each strip in the same way as you would when making bias binding (see page 123). Set your stitch length back to normal and stitch along the long unfolded edge to secure. Feed one tie through each casing and knot at the sides to secure.

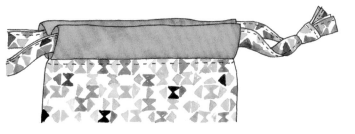

finishing Snip away all remaining thread ends to neaten. Fold the blanket neatly into thirds, slip it into the bag, and draw up the ties.

colorful cot quilt

A quilt is often described as a cuddle you can keep— and when you wrap your little one up in this handmade blanket, you'll see why! The combination of bright colors and monochrome prints is perfect for young babies.

YOU WILL NEED

- 8–12 fat quarters in a range of different colors
- 40 x 45 in. (100 x 115 cm) print cotton for the backing
- 40 x 45 in. (100 x 115 cm) batting (wadding)
- 5 yd. (4.6 m) ready-made quilt binding, 2 in. (5 cm) deep (or make your own)
- Coordinating thread
- Sewing machine
- Iron
- Rotary cutter, cutting mat, and ruler
- Pins
- Fabric marking pencil or tailor's chalk
- Hand sewing needle

SIZE

33 x 37 in. (84 x 94 cm)

PATTERN NOTE

Take a ¼-in. (5-mm) seam allowance throughout unless otherwise stated.

PATTERN PIECES REQUIRED

None

MAKE IT YOURS

You can create a super-cozy quilt by using a brushed cotton or even minky fabric as the quilt backing.

1 From the fat quarters cut 72 5-in. (12.5-cm) squares, selecting different colors at random. Pin them right sides together in unmatching pairs. Using the ruler and fabric marking pencil or tailor's chalk, draw a diagonal line from one corner to the other. Do this with all the pairs of squares.

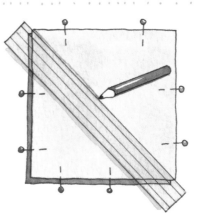

2 Machine stitch diagonally across each square, stitching ¼ in. (5 mm) from each side of the marked line.

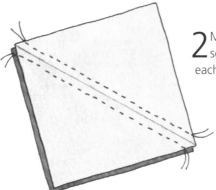

3 Using the rotary cutter and ruler on a cutting mat, cut down the marked line to give two squares made of half-square triangles in different colors. Press the seams open. Repeat with all the remaining squares to create 72 half-square triangle blocks.

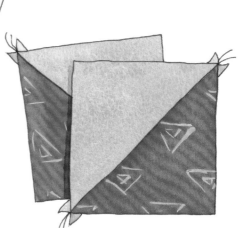

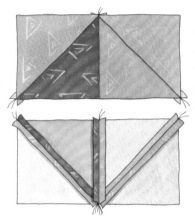

4 Arrange the squares in nine rows of eight, moving the colors and turning the patches around until you are happy with the way it all looks. With right sides together, pin and stitch the squares together in pairs, then join the pairs into rows, pressing the seams open as you work. Once you've assembled all nine rows, join the rows together and press the seams open.

5 Place the backing fabric wrong side up on your work surface, with the quilt batting (wadding) on top. Center the completed quilt top on the batting—there will be a border of approximately 4 in. (10 cm) of backing fabric and batting all around. Pin and baste (tack) the three layers together.

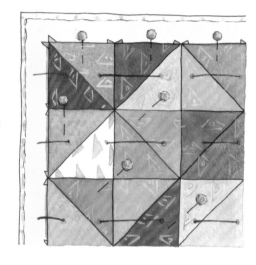

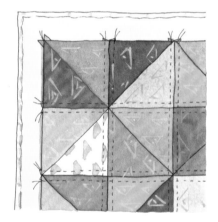

6 Now quilt the piece by working vertical lines of stitching on each side of the seams between the squares, stitching ½ in. (approx. 1 cm) from the seam. Start from the center and work outward on alternate sides in turn. Then turn the quilt through 90° and repeat the quilting process, again working from the center out. Remove the basting stitches.

7 Using the rotary cutter mat and ruler, neatly trim away the excess batting and backing from the quilt, squaring the quilt as you work.

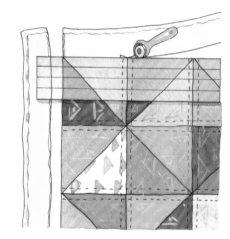

TIP *Make your own binding by cutting strips 2 in. (5 cm) deep across the width of the fabric, joining them together to make the required length, and pressing creases as shown on page 123.*

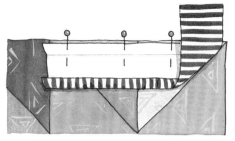

8 With the quilt top right side up, open out the length of binding, align the raw edge with the raw edge of the quilt, and pin in place. When you get to the corner of the first side, fold the binding up away from the quilt, aligning the raw edges with the next side to be stitched.

9 Fold the binding back down to align with the next side to be stitched; this will create a small triangle that sits over the corner of the quilt. When you've pinned all sides, overlap the ends of the binding, tucking the raw edges neatly inside, and sew the binding in place, positioning the stitches just inside the crease nearest the raw edge of the binding.

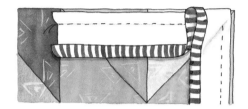

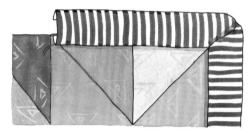

10 Fold the binding over to the backing, to conceal the raw edges. Neaten the miters over each of the corners and pin in place.

TIP Don't stitch around the quilt in a continuous line. Instead, measure the distance from the edge of the binding to the first crease line; on each side of the quilt, start and stop your stitching this distance away from the edge of the quilt.

11 Slipstitch the binding to the backing of the quilt to finish.

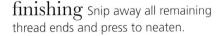

finishing Snip away all remaining thread ends and press to neaten.

techniques

The sewing techniques in this book are all very simple—ideal for making quick-and-easy garments and accessories for kids!

WORKING WITH PATTERNS AND TEMPLATES

The garment patterns on the pull-out sheets at the back of this book are printed to their actual size. To use them, you will need to trace them from the sheets onto tracing paper, greaseproof paper, or pattern paper, which is available from sewing and haberdashery stores. (Whatever you use, check that it is thin enough to see through.) Trace the pieces in the size that you need (the pattern guide shows you which line to follow) and cut them out.

Each pattern piece includes a seam allowance of ⅜ in. (1 cm). The seam allowance is the distance from the outer edge that indicates where the stitching line should be.

On pages 124–6 you will find templates for some of the smaller accessories and pieces such as patch pockets. Some of these are full size, so you can just trace them onto paper, cut them out, and pin them to your chosen fabric; some are printed at 50%, so you will need to enlarge them by 200% on a photocopier first before tracing and cutting out.

POSITIONING PATTERN PIECES ON THE FABRIC

In dressmaking, the vast majority of pattern pieces need to be cut from a double layer of fabric. You generally have to fold your fabric in a particular way before you pin the pattern pieces to it and cut them out. There are three main ways of folding the fabric (see below); the project instructions will tell you which one to follow.

Many pattern pieces are symmetrical—the back of a bodice or shirt, for example. Instead of being cut as one

huge paper pattern, these pieces are often cut out as a half piece and the center line is placed on the fold of the fabric. A double-headed arrow on a pattern indicates an edge that has to be placed on the fold.

Sometimes you may have two pieces that are the same shape but need to be mirror images of each other—the left and right sides of a shirt front, for example. If you're cutting these from a doubled layer of fabric, there's no problem—the two pieces will automatically be mirror

Fold in half widthwise, matching up the selvages.

Fold both selvages in to meet in the center.

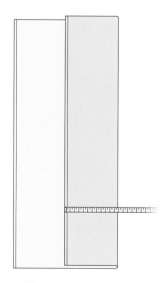

Fold one or both selvages in toward the center, just far enough to accommodate the specified pattern piece(s).

TIP *Some people fold their fabric right sides together and pin the pattern pieces to the wrong side. I prefer to fold my fabric wrong sides together, so that I can make any marks such as buttonhole positions on the right side of the fabric. This also makes it easier to match patterns—for example, if you want horizontal stripes or checks to align across the front and back of a garment.*

images when they're cut out. But if you're cutting them from a single layer of fabric, you must remember to flip the pattern over before you cut out the second piece so that you get a left- and a right-hand piece.

Fold the fabric in the way specified in the instructions, then pin the pattern pieces in place, draw around them with tailor's chalk, and cut out.

The illustrations of pattern layouts in the projects are intended only as a rough guide: lay out all the pattern pieces on your fabric before you begin cutting to make sure you're using the most economical layout and avoid wasting fabric. If you're using a print and want to match the pattern across two adjoining pieces, you may also find that you need to move the pieces around slightly to get the best result.

The fabric quantities given should be sufficient for the largest size of each garment, but you should allow more for fabrics with a nap, or to match patterns. You may also be able to use slightly less or narrower fabric for the smaller sizes—experiment with the layout before you buy.

TRANSFERRING PATTERN MARKS TO THE FABRIC

Patterns are marked to show where to position features like pockets, buttonholes, and other fastenings, or where you need to work rows of gathering stitches. Transfer any markings to the fabric before you unpin the pattern pieces. You can do this using either a chalk pencil, or tailor's tacks.

If you're using a chalk pencil, make a small hole in the pattern and mark the position on the fabric. If your fabric is folded, push a pin straight sown through the fabric at the marked point, and then mark the position on the bottom layer of fabric.

To work a tailor's tack, thread the needle with a double loop of cotton in a contrasting color to your fabric, but do not knot the ends. At the marked point on the pattern, take the needle down through the fabric and back up again, and then repeat the process through the same stitch to leave a loop on the surface of the fabric. Leave a tail of thread on each side and do not draw the loop tight. When you remove the paper pattern, the tack will remain on the surface of the fabric as a position guide. If the tailor's tack is worked over two layers of fabric, gently pull the layers apart and cut through the threads of the loop in the center; this will leave the threads of the tack stitching on both pieces of fabric.

DOUBLE-TURNED HEM

Double hemming gives a very neat finish and will prevent fraying.

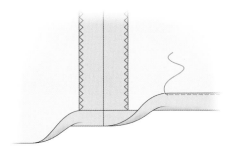

Following the measurements specified in the project, fold the edge of the fabric over to the wrong side and press. Fold over again, pin, baste (tack), press, and machine stitch in place, stitching as close as possible to the folded edge.

GATHERING

Gathers are small, soft folds formed by drawing the fabric into a smaller area. They are a lovely way of adding fullness to a garment, as in the Gathered Skirt on page 60.

Gathering by machine

Machine gathering is done by stitching two rows of long machine stitches along the edge to be gathered and then pulling the bobbin threads.

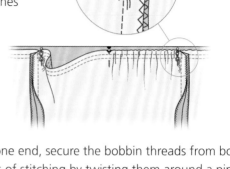

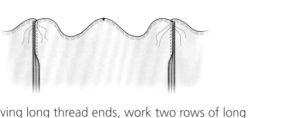

1 Leaving long thread ends, work two rows of long machine stitches ¼ in. (6 mm) apart along the edge to be gathered, within the seam allowance.

2 At one end, secure the bobbin threads from both lines of stitching by twisting them around a pin in a figure-eight. At the other end, pull both bobbin threads together and gently ease the gathers along the threads. When you have gathered the fabric to the required length, secure the thread ends around another pin.

3 Unwind the thread ends from the end pins and knot each pair together; trim the ends.

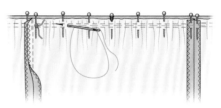

4 With the gathered side on top, pin and baste (tack) the gathered piece to the corresponding garment piece. Remove the pins.

Gathering by hand

Gathering fabric by hand is very easy to do—and on small items such as children's clothing, it is also very quick. Start by making several tiny backstitches to fasten the thread securely at one end of the section to be gathered. Sew a row of small, evenly spaced running stitches just above the seam line, then sew a second row parallel to the first, just below the seam line. Pull up the two loose threads and distribute the fullness evenly until the section is the desired length. Attach the loose threads around a pin at the finishing end (see step 2 of Gathering by machine).

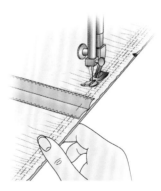

5 Set your stitch length back to normal. With the gathered edge on top, machine stitch the gathered edge to the corresponding edge, reverse stitching to start and finish. Remove the basting stitches.

BINDING

Binding is used in several projects in this book. To bind straight edges, strips of fabric cut on the straight of grain can be used. To bind curves (around a neckline, for example), you will need to cut fabric strips on the bias.

Making bias binding

1 Using a ruler and chalk, mark lines about 2 in. (5 cm) apart at a 45-degree angle across the fabric and cut along them.

2 To join strips together, cut the two ends that are to be joined at a 45-degree angle. Place one strip on top of the other, right sides together, and stitch the pieces together diagonally.

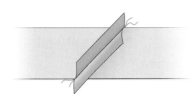

3 Press the seam open and trim the excess from the sides, in line with the edges of the strip. Continue to join the strips together until the bias strip is the length you need for your project.

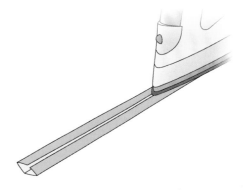

4 With wrong sides together, fold the strip in half widthwise and press. Open out the central crease, then fold each long edge of the binding in to meet at the central crease and press again.

ELASTICATED WAISTBAND OR CASING

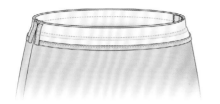  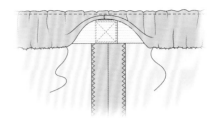

1 With wrong sides together, press a center fold along the length of the waistband, then open it out again. Turn under ¼ in. (5 mm) along the long bottom edge and press. With right sides together, pin and stitch the short ends of the waistband together to form a loop. Press the seam open. With right sides together, aligning the waistband seam with the center back seam of the garment, pin and stitch the unpressed long edge around the waist. Press the seam allowance up, toward the waistband.

2 Turn the waistband over to the inside of the garment along the center crease line, so that the pressed-under bottom edge covers the previous seam line, and slipstitch around, leaving a 1½ in. (4-cm) gap at the center back. Attach a safety pin to one end of the elastic and feed it through the waistband. Once the elastic is fed through, pull both ends out of the waistband and overlap them by 1 in. (2.5 cm) to accommodate the child's waist measurements.

3 Stitch the ends of the elastic together by stitching around the overlapped area in a square, finishing at the starting point with the needle down. Pivot the work around the needle and stitch diagonally across the square, then along the adjacent side of the square and diagonally across to the opposite corner. This is known as "box stitching." Allow the elastic to slip back inside the waistband. Slipstitch the gap closed.

templates

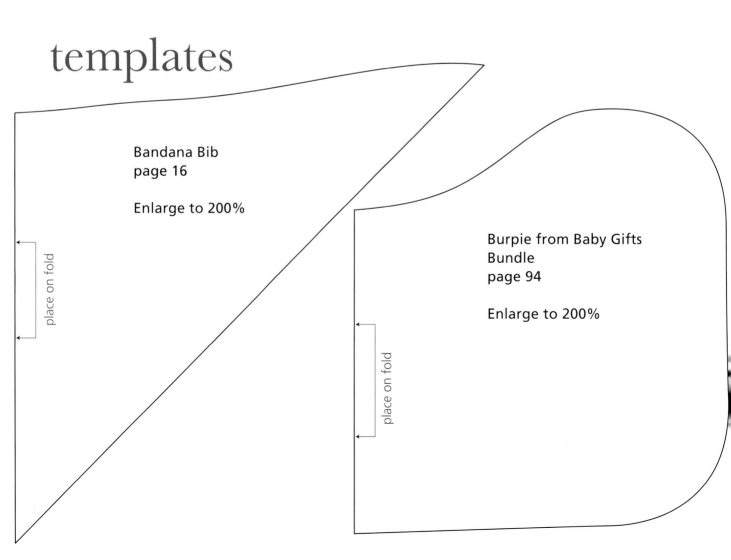

Bandana Bib
page 16

Enlarge to 200%

place on fold

Burpie from Baby Gifts Bundle
page 94

Enlarge to 200%

place on fold

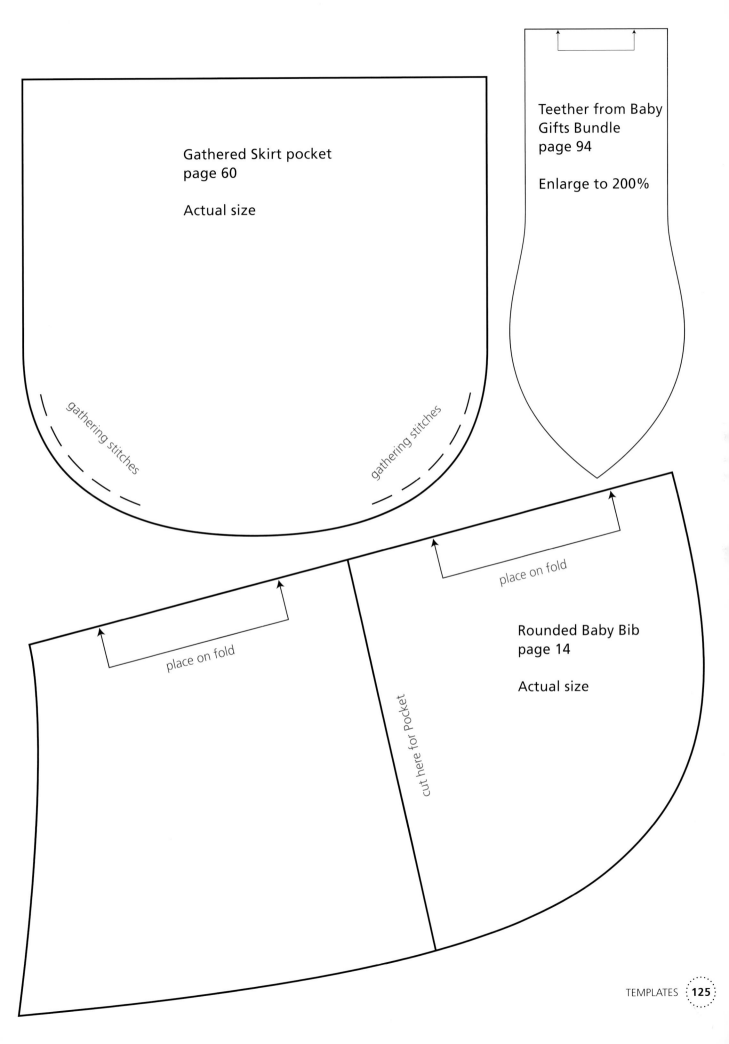

Gathered Skirt pocket
page 60

Actual size

gathering stitches

gathering stitches

Teether from Baby
Gifts Bundle
page 94

Enlarge to 200%

place on fold

place on fold

cut here for Pocket

Rounded Baby Bib
page 14

Actual size

Knotted Headband
page 108

Enlarge to 200%

place on fold

Bunny body
page 102

Actual size

Bunny ear
page 102

Actual size

Bunny arm
page 102

Actual size

index

suppliers

When it comes to making clothing and accessories for babies and children, modern stitchers are spoilt for choice—there are so many wonderful fabrics to choose from, in a range of finishes from pure cottons to easy-care blends, stretch knits, and cozy flannels. You can build your stash with a selection of bold bright solids and team them with fun colorful prints. Here are some fantastic suppliers to get you started on building your stitching stash!

Abakhan
www.abakhan.co.uk

Art Gallery Fabrics
www.artgalleryfabrics.com
www.guthrie-ghani.co.uk
www.eternalmaker.com

Cloud 9 Fabrics
www.cloud9fabrics.com
www.misformake.co.uk

Dashwood
www.dashwoodstudio.com

Jo-Ann Fabric and Craft Stores
www.joann.com

John Lewis
www.johnlewis.com

Michaels
www.michaels.com

Simply Solids
www.simplysolids.co.uk

Vlieseline
www.vlieseline.com

acknowledgments

I'm so proud of this collection of stitched baby garments and extend my thanks to Cindy Richards, Penny Craig, Miriam Catley, and the team at CICO Books—from editors and illustrators, to photographers and stylists—it is a joy to work with such a fabulous team!

I would also like to thank Dashwood Studios, Art Gallery Fabrics, and Cloud 9 Fabrics for their phenomenal support with this collection.

Thank you to the online stitching community, friends and readers of my blog www.madepeachy.com. I hope that you love this book as much as I loved making it!

I am blessed with family and friends, that are not only supportive but are truly encouraging, who are always there to cheer me on—thank you!

Finally, John, my husband, thank you for always having faith in me and making me smile every day!

HOW TO USE THE PULL-OUT PATTERNS—PLEASE READ CAREFULLY

The patterns in the pull-out section (opposite) are full size, so you do not need to enlarge them. You will need to copy the patterns onto tracing paper, parchment, or dressmaker's pattern paper and then cut out, that way they can be reused again and again. (Dressmaker's pattern paper or tracing paper is available from sewing stores or online suppliers.) The key shows which lines you need to follow for the different ages. Seam allowances are included; check the text for each project, as some measurements may vary. Also, check the pattern labeling carefully to ensure you trace off the correct line that corresponds to your required age and size.

Some of the patterns are shown as halves. When you come to cut out these pieces of fabric, fold the material as instructed in the text and align the PLACE ON FOLD line on the pattern with the fold in the fabric.

Where there are left and right sides to a garment piece—for example, the left and right front of a shirt—cut one side, then flip the pattern over before you pin it to the fabric and cut the second side.